40 Days to
Peace and Union
with God

LENT CYCLE A

40 Days to Peace and Union with God

A Journey in Prayer
Through the Daily Gospels

Reflections by Fr. John Bartunek, L.C., Th.D.

Introduction by Fr. John Bartunek & Dan Burke

SOPHIA INSTITUTE PRESS
Manchester, New Hampshire

Sophia Institute Press
Box 5284, Manchester, NH 03108
1-800-888-9344
www.SophiaInstitute.com

Sophia Institute Press is a registered trademark of Sophia Institute.

paperback ISBN 978-1-64413-997-4

ebook ISBN 978-1-64413-998-1

LCCN: 2023930203

CONTENTS

40 Days to
Peace and Union
with God

INTRODUCTION

Authentic Christian prayer is nothing less than a conversation with God — with the One who created us in love and for love. It is an ongoing interaction that gives us a chance to know God better and provides God with the invitation He desires to touch our souls with His healing grace. That's the real source of inner strength and wisdom that we need so that we can find and follow God's plan for our lives. And following His plan is the only way to find lasting peace and union with God, both here on earth and in Heaven.

The challenge we all face is that our lives are so noisy that this communion with God easily breaks down or falls by the wayside. This is why we created this forty-day challenge to deeper prayer, peace, and union with God. When you pray with *40 Days to Peace and Union with God,*[1] you are committing to do your part, and if you do your part, you can be assured that God will do His — because God is faithful. As the Holy Spirit beckons us through St. James, "Draw near to God, and He will draw near to you" (4:8, NABRE).

Christians who take their faith seriously pray. Authentic disciples of Jesus pray. Their typical days, weeks, months, and years are seasoned with prayer: traditional prayers, liturgical prayers, spontaneous prayers, the Rosary. Authentic disciples make prayer commitments, giving structure and consistency to their faith journey. These commitments and this dedication

---

[1]   The Lenten Gospel readings and meditations in this book cover the Liturgical Year Cycle A. The Sunday Gospel readings for Year A are mainly taken from Matthew's Gospel.

to prayer and relationship with God keep Christians united to the Vine, so their lives can bear the fruit both they and Christ long for.

Among the most foundational and powerful prayer commitments is one that can have more bearing on your life than any other because it is more personalized: *daily mental prayer.* There is no saint in Heaven who has failed to draw near to Jesus daily with this kind of prayer. Mental prayer is the prayer of saints — but it is not beyond those who desire to become saints. Instead, it is the pathway to our high calling to become saints. It is the way in which Jesus leads us to union with Him and to finding peace, passion, and purpose in life.

No book can pray for you. No book can teach you to pray. At most, a book can be a useful tool to lead you to prayer as a new discipline or lead you deeper into prayer if you are already a practiced dedicated friend of Jesus. *40 Days to Peace and Union with God* is designed to help you engage more actively in the quest of daily mental prayer so you can reap more fruits of spiritual growth.

This book will help you in several key ways. First, it provides a simple structure for prayer that you may not yet have in place. Second, it provides daily inspirations to stir the thirsty heart to prayer. Finally, it provides a connection to thousands of others who will join in this beautiful symphony of love lifted by the hearts of God's people — by *your* heart — to His eternal praise in Heaven.

We have no doubt that if you give your heart to this challenge, you will never be the same and will better know the peace and presence of God in your life. We would also like to offer help in the form of an online video series that you can sign up for at https://spiritualdirection.com/into-the-deep. There is no doubt you can do this, and you are not alone!

Now, let's dive into a simple but powerful approach to prayer and this forty-day adventure into grace.

In this basic approach to prayer, here are a few secrets to consider to help you succeed during these forty days and beyond:

Sacred time: It is very powerful and helpful to make a commitment to God regarding the time you will give to Him in prayer each day. Simply determine how much time you will give to this prayer commitment each day and when. As you will see, it is very brief, so ten minutes should be more than enough. The key is to show up at the same time every day so that your body becomes your friend as you build or deepen your habit of prayer. Once you decide the time and the duration, then simply make a firm commitment to the Lord and ask for His help so that you can fulfill your promise.

Sacred space: It can be very helpful to set aside a special place where you will pray each day. It need not be elaborate or expensive. You can use a candle, your favorite icon, a holy card, a crucifix, or whatever helps you to focus your heart and mind on God. Coupled with your sacred time, this space will provide helpful motivation, rhythm, and encouragement to pray, especially on those tough days when your motivation might not be as strong.

Just show up: No matter how you feel, how well you pray, or even whether you are able to stay awake! God will honor your presence whenever you simply do your best to draw near to Him. He will never fail to keep His end of the promise and will even make up for your lack of ability to pray. He makes this promise in Romans chapter 8, where He reveals that when we come to pray but struggle, He will pray in us! What an amazing gift! So on the worst days, we just need to show up, and He will take care of the rest.

No condemnation: Saints know that the perfect can often get in the way of the good for people who have a deep desire to honor God. We can't let our perfectionism or self-condemnation get in the way of our relationship with God. If we fail to show up when we should because we were up too late the night before, we should just ask for forgiveness, reaffirm our commitment, and move forward. Another powerful practice is to take these failures to Confession, not only to receive forgiveness but also to receive the grace to help us keep our commitments. As the Father of the prodigal son, God is always looking for us to return, and He is ready to receive us and help us when we do.

YOUR THREE-STEP GUIDE TO
DAILY MENTAL PRAYER

READY

Find a quiet place. Turn off and set aside your phone, computer — everything. Close your eyes or look at something beautiful in nature or religious art. Remind yourself that God is with you, within you, or right beside you, eager to have this conversation with you. Express your gratitude that He has called you to pray and that He is present with you now.

SET

Thank God for a blessing that He has given you. It could be a little one or a big one, from yesterday or from a long time ago.

Ask God for something that you or someone you care about really needs.

Open your heart to hear His Word: "Speak, Lord, your servant is listening" (1 Sam. 3:10, NABRE).

GO

Read: Read each Gospel passage attentively, slowly — word by word. Reading out loud can help you to slow things down. Pay attention to every word.

KEY QUESTIONS: What does the Bible text say in itself? What did the author intend? What does the Church teach about this subject?

Reflect: Reflect prayerfully, engaging with the meaning of the passage and considering how it may apply to your life circumstances.

KEY QUESTIONS: What does this text say to me? How does it apply to my life? Where is God leading me? What is He revealing to me?

Respond: Converse with God about the passage.

KEY QUESTIONS: What can I say in response to God? Should I offer thanksgiving or praise, or should I ask for His help in any particular way? Should I ask for forgiveness?

Rest: Let yourself rest and remain absorbed in the words of God, allowing or inviting the Holy Spirit to draw you more deeply into His presence through what you've read. Whenever God touches our hearts in any way as we read, we should rest and allow His presence to wash over us until it fades; and then we can read the passage again. We repeat this cycle until the movement is completely gone.

KEY QUESTIONS: Am I being patient, attentive, and open to God's movement in my soul as I rest in His self-revelation?

Resolve: Allow the encounter with God to permeate your day, causing you to draw ever nearer to Him through His self-revelation and His invitation to participate with Him in making His presence known in the world.

KEY QUESTIONS: What can I specifically do to respond to what God has revealed to me in this passage? How can I carry this encounter with me into the day to influence how I think and act? Write down your resolutions and conclude with a prayer of thanksgiving.

You can pray your own closing prayer of thanksgiving or use the one included[2] below, but be sure to *mean* what you say as you pray it slowly and deliberately. Remember, this is a *conversation* with God.

We will remain united in prayer with you,
Fr. John Bartunek, LC
Dan Burke, Founder, Avila Institute

[2] Please earmark the closing prayer on the following page to use at the end of your prayer time each day.

CLOSING PRAYER OF THANKSGIVING

Most Blessed and Holy Trinity, Father, Son, and Holy Spirit, thank You for Your love and Your grace in allowing me this time of prayer with You

The world, the flesh, and the devil will all propose things I should focus on and run after today. I beg You to fill me with Your Holy Spirit and help me instead to know and embrace Your will. Help me to see what You desire of me each moment of this day. Give me the wisdom, strength, and fortitude I need to avoid distractions, discern Your will, and focus on and carry out that which Wisdom reveals. Help me to work and live at a pace of peace and prayerfulness, always attentive to You, able to hear Your voice and to say no to anything that hinders my journey to You and a complete yes to every Holy prompting from You.

Help me to humbly and purposefully live, light, and lead others to the path of union with You and to tell everyone about this way of life. Amen.

DAY 1
ASH WEDNESDAY

THE SECRET RENDEZVOUS

"But there is another and interior way of praying without ceasing, and that is the way of desire. Whatever else you are doing, if you long for that Sabbath, you are not ceasing to pray. If you do not want to cease praying, do not cease longing. Your unceasing desire is your unceasing voice." ~ST. AUGUSTINE

READ: MATTHEW 6:1-6, 16-18

"Be careful not to parade your good deeds before men to attract their notice; by doing this you will lose all reward from your Father in heaven. So when you give alms, do not have it trumpeted before you; this is what the hypocrites do in the synagogues and in the streets to win men's admiration. I tell you solemnly, they have had their reward. But when you give alms, your left hand must not know what your right is doing; your almsgiving must be secret, and your Father who sees all that is done in secret will reward you. And when you pray, do not imitate the hypocrites: they love to say their prayers standing up in the synagogues and at the street corners for people to see them; I tell you solemnly, they have had their reward. But when you pray, go to your private room and, when you have shut your door, pray to your Father who is in that secret place, and your Father who sees all that is done in secret will reward you.... When you fast do not put on a gloomy look as the hypocrites do: they pull long faces to let men know they are fasting. I tell you solemnly, they have had their reward. But when you fast, put oil on your head and wash your face, so that no one will know you are fasting except your Father who sees all that is done in secret; and your Father who sees all that is done in secret will reward you."

REFLECT

Hidden behind this sobering lesson against the temptation of hypocrisy is a beautiful revelation of the heart of Christ. He points out that He sees "what is done in secret." He repeats this three times. He has seen all of the most selfish, vitriolic, and morose chapters of each of our ongoing interior monologues — everything. He knows it all. And yet He still loves us with the tender love of the perfect father, the perfect friend. If this doesn't prove what unconditional love really is, nothing does.

But it doesn't stop there. He wants us to let Him into that monologue, to turn it into an ongoing dialogue, a conversation with Him. He wants to take part in everything we do; He wants to be our closest companion, our most intimate friend. And why? Because He has some psychological need that we can pacify for Him? No. Just the opposite. Because He has more that He wants to give us. He has a reward to give each one of us, the reward of our true name (see Rev. 2:17), our fulfillment, the satisfaction of our deepest yearnings — most of all, He wants to give us Himself, now and for all eternity.

RESPOND

You see all my motives and intentions, but I think sometimes I try to hide from them. Show them to me, Lord. I don't want anything to get in the way of our friendship. I don't want to fall into hypocrisy. I want to do all things out of a humble, sincere love for You. With the humility of Your heart, Lord, shape my heart.

REST

At times, life seems so complicated, but You simplify it. Stay with me, Lord; walk with me; teach me how to love You, to love my neighbor, and to master my selfish tendencies. With the silence of Your heart, speak to my heart.

RESOLVE

How can I carry this encounter with me into the day? (Write / Journal)

CLOSING PRAYER OF THANKSGIVING

Turn to page 9

DAY 2
THURSDAY

CROSSES WITH CHRIST

"The only petition I would have you put forward on my behalf is that I may be given sufficient inward and outward strength to be as resolute in will as in words, and a Christian in reality instead of only in repute." ~ST. IGNATIUS OF ANTIOCH

READ: LUKE 9:18–27

Now one day when he was praying alone in the presence of his disciples he put this question to them, "Who do the crowds say I am?" And they answered, "John the Baptist; others Elijah; and others say one of the ancient prophets come back to life." "But you," he said, "who do you say I am?" It was Peter who spoke up. "The Christ of God," he said. But he gave them strict orders not to tell anyone anything about this. "The Son of Man," he said, "is destined to suffer grievously, to be rejected by the elders and chief priests and scribes and to be put to death, and to be raised up on the third day." Then to all he said, "If anyone wants to be a follower of mine, let him renounce himself and take up his cross every day and follow me. For anyone who wants to save his life will lose it; but anyone who loses his life for my sake, that man will save it. What gain, then, is it for a man to have won the whole world and to have lost or ruined his very self? For if anyone is ashamed of me and of my words, of him the Son of Man will be ashamed when he comes in his own glory and in the glory of the Father and the holy angels. I tell you truly, there are some standing here who will not taste death before they see the kingdom of God."

REFLECT

True friends tell friends the hard truth; flatterers don't. In this intimate exchange, Jesus looks His chosen disciples in the eye and tells them a very hard truth — that their lives will take on real meaning only if they are willing to sacrifice whatever is necessary (dreams, hopes, comfort, plans) in order to follow Him. If we don't take the time to learn this lesson, we run the risk of discarding our friendship with Christ when it starts to cost us. Jesus warns us that if we are ashamed of Him and our identification with Him, if we prefer acceptance by the world and worldly success to being a faithful Christian, then we may, tragically, end up with what we have preferred. In the end, Christ's Kingdom will come in all its glory (now in the Church, it is still in embryonic form), and our allegiance to Him, in spite of suffering and rejection, will prove to have been, as He promises us, the wiser course. If Christ had not traveled that path ahead of us, climbing the hill of Calvary and dying on a cross, it would be hard to believe Him. But He has, and so it shouldn't be that hard after all.

RESPOND

And if You were to ask me this question: "Who do you say I am?," how would I answer? I would say the right words: "You are the Messiah, the Son of God, the Lord of life and history." But I think You would keep looking at me, because You see beyond words into my heart. And in my heart, Lord, I have still not surrendered completely to Your love. Lord Jesus, help me.

REST

What are You asking of me, Lord? Okay, I give it to You. I will follow where You lead. If You went to Calvary for me, I will go there for You. Help me to see everything with faith. If I know it's Your will, I can embrace it, but my faith is sometimes so weak that I forget to look for Your hand in the circumstances and responsibilities of my life. Lord, increase my faith.

RESOLVE

How can I carry this encounter with me into the day? (Write / Journal)

CLOSING PRAYER OF THANKSGIVING

Turn to page 9

DAY 3
FRIDAY

NEW WINE AT THE WEDDING

"God's splendor is the source of life, those who see him share his life. Because he was beyond the reach of man's mind, incomprehensible and invisible, he made himself visible, intelligible and knowable so that those who see and accept him may possess life." ~ST. IRENAEUS

READ: MATTHEW 9:14-17

Then John's disciples came to him and said, "Why is it that we and the Pharisees fast, but your disciples do not?" Jesus replied, "Surely the bridegroom's attendants would never think of mourning as long as the bridegroom is still with them? But the time will come for the bridegroom to be taken away from them, and then they will fast. No one puts a piece of unshrunken cloth onto an old cloak, because the patch pulls away from the cloak and the tear gets worse. Nor do people put new wine into old wineskins; if they do, the skins burst, the wine runs out, and the skins are lost. No; they put new wine into fresh skins and both are preserved."

REFLECT

Jesus wants to come into your life because He wants you to share His joy. He calls His disciples His "wedding guests." The Greek term literally means "children of the bridal chamber," a phrase that referred to those special guests who were the bridegroom's best friends, the ones who spent the weeklong wedding reception (the ancient Palestinian alternative to modern-day honeymoons) at his side, sharing his joy and celebrating with him. Jesus wants your friendship, and He wants it to deepen, so that the indescribable joy that overflows from His love can spill into your life and the lives of those around you. He only needs you to say one thing to make it happen — but He needs you to say it over and over: "Jesus, Thy will be done."

RESPOND

I know, Lord, that a sad saint is a bad saint. You are a God of joy. I long for true joy, the kind that lasts even in the midst of suffering, because it is grounded in Your love, a love that never tires. I believe in Your love, Jesus, but I still need You to teach me how to live in its light. You are the bridegroom of my heart. Teach me the way to go; show me the path to follow. Sometimes I am afraid of what You might ask me. Like John the Baptist's disciples, I hesitate to follow You. Why, Lord? Enlighten me. Your will is full of wisdom. Give me the courage to be wise.

REST

You guide all of history. You prepared the world for the Incarnation, and now You spread Your grace slowly but surely through the work of Your Church. Thank You for Your presence, Your forgiveness, and Your grace. I want to build Your Church, to be a healthy cell in the Body of Christ. Make use of me, Lord. With You, I can do all things.

RESOLVE

How can I carry this encounter with me into the day? (Write / Journal)

CLOSING PRAYER OF THANKSGIVING

Turn to page 9

DAY 4
SATURDAY

MAKING ALL THINGS NEW

"As the tree is known by its fruits, so they who claim to belong to Christ are known by their actions; for this work of ours does not consist in just making professions, but in a faith that is both practical and lasting." ~ST. IGNATIUS OF ANTIOCH

READ: LUKE 5:27-39

When he went out after this, he noticed a tax collector, Levi by name, sitting by the customs house, and said to him, "Follow me." And leaving everything he got up and followed him. In his honor Levi held a great reception in his house, and with them at table was a large gathering of tax collectors and others. The Pharisees and their scribes complained to his disciples and said, "Why do you eat and drink with tax collectors and sinners?" Jesus said to them in reply, "It is not those who are well who need the doctor, but the sick. I have not come to call the virtuous, but sinners to repentance." They then said to him, "John's disciples are always fasting and saying prayers, and the disciples of the Pharisees too, but yours go on eating and drinking." Jesus replied, "Surely you cannot make the bridegroom's attendants fast while the bridegroom is still with them? But the time will come, the time for the bridegroom to be taken away from them; that will be the time when they will fast." He also told them this parable, "No one tears a piece from a new cloak to put it on an old cloak; if he does, not only will he have torn the new one, but the piece taken from the new will not match the old. And nobody puts new wine into old skins; if he does, the new wine will burst the skins and then run out, and the skins will be lost. No; new wine must be put into fresh skins. And nobody who has been drinking old wine wants new. 'The old is good,' he says."

REFLECT

St. Luke paints a vivid picture of the encounter between Jesus and Levi. Jesus is walking downtown, probably with His disciples, and sees Levi there at his office. Luke says that Jesus "noticed a tax collector, Levi by name." Isn't it just like Jesus to notice someone — what a torrent of instruction rushes out of that one little verb! It means that the Lord is always on the lookout. It means that Jesus is thinking not of Himself but of us and of our needs. It means that He recognizes the needs and desires and yearnings of our hearts. Jesus notices this unhappy tax collector, a social pariah, and calls him, renews his life, and gives him a mission and a meaning.

That's what Jesus does. He is the doctor of every soul; He detects our every need and hope, and He prescribes the perfect medicine. He is the bridegroom of every heart; He gazes on us with personal, determined love and leads us into the everlasting adventure of indescribable intimacy and communion with God. Jesus is a friend, true — but what a friend He is, and what great friends He teaches us to be!

RESPOND

Lord, sometimes I wonder why You keep asking me for more, why You keep sending me more crosses, more missions. Why can't we relax and take it easy? I know the answer: because You love me too much, and You love every person too much — You suffered and died to win us grace, and You want that grace to fill us and lead us to true meaning and lasting happiness. Lord Jesus, I trust in You.

REST

I remember the first time I heard Your voice in my heart. I was like Levi, living an average life, wanting more but not knowing where to find it. And You noticed me. You notice me every day, every moment. Give me a heart like Yours, one that responds, like Levi, to Your every wish and, in turn, reaches out to others as You have reached out to me. Teach me, Lord.

RESOLVE

How can I carry this encounter with me into the day? (Write / Journal)

CLOSING PRAYER OF THANKSGIVING

Turn to page 9

DAY 5
FIRST SUNDAY OF LENT

DESERT STORM

"Lord of the universe, he hid his infinite glory
and took the nature of a servant. Incapable of
suffering as God, he did not refuse to be a man,
capable of suffering." ~POPE ST. LEO THE GREAT

READ. MATTHEW 4:1-11

Then Jesus was led by the Spirit out into the wilderness to be tempted by
the devil. He fasted for forty days and forty nights, after which he was very
hungry, and the tempter came and said to him, "If you are the Son of God,
tell these stones to turn into loaves." But he replied, "Scripture says: Man
does not live on bread alone but on every word that comes from the mouth
of God." The devil then took him to the holy city and made him stand on the
parapet of the Temple. "If you are the Son of God," he said, "throw yourself
down; for scripture says: He will put you in his angels' charge, and they will
support you on their hands in case you hurt your foot against a stone." Jesus
said to him, "Scripture also says: You must not put the Lord your God to
the test." Next, taking him to a very high mountain, the devil showed him
all the kingdoms of the world and their splendor. "I will give you all these,"
he said, "if you fall at my feet and worship me." Then Jesus replied, "Be off,
Satan! For scripture says: You must worship the Lord your God, and serve
him alone." Then the devil left him, and angels appeared and looked after him.

REFLECT

Jesus Christ knows what it means to suffer temptation. He is truly human,
just like us in all things except sin. Therefore, we can appeal to Him when
temptations beset us; He knows what we are going through. He did not
want to leave us alone in our struggles; He wishes to walk by our side every
step along the way. That's why He came to earth in the first place. In Christ,

we have a friend like no other: His patience is boundless, His empathy is complete, and His concern for us is as personal as it is pure.

> *Jesus: Do not be afraid — even when you are weak and you fall, I will be there to pick you up. Trust in the strength of prayer and sacrifice, and no temptations will drag you away from me. To be tempted doesn't mean to deny me — just turn your gaze back to me, and I will be there to strengthen you against the wiles of the devil. In the desert, the thought of you spurred me on. I wanted to suffer in the wilderness to convince you that I can be there to hold you and guide you in the dark nights of your soul. I am with you until the end of time.*

RESPOND

Lord, Your motto was so simple: "Thy will be done." I want to live by the same motto. But I often follow other mottos, other desires. Teach me how to close the gap between what I want to be (Your faithful follower) and what I too often am (self-seeking, self-absorbed, self-indulgent). With the Kingdom of Your heart, reign in my heart.

REST

You have done so much for me, Lord. And I forget so easily. You suffered for me — just for me. You were tempted, You fasted, You were hungry — all for me, to save me, to redeem me. Thank You, Lord. What would You have me do?

RESOLVE

How can I carry this encounter with me into the day? (Write / Journal)

CLOSING PRAYER OF THANKSGIVING

Turn to page 9

DAY 6
MONDAY

CHEAT SHEET

"I beg you, join with me in love. Run with me in faith. Let us yearn for our heavenly home. Let us sigh for it. Let us realize that we are strangers here below." ~ST. AUGUSTINE

READ: MATTHEW 25:31-46

"When the Son of Man comes in his glory, escorted by all the angels, then he will take his seat on his throne of glory. All the nations will be assembled before him and he will separate men one from another as the shepherd separates sheep from goats. He will place the sheep on his right hand and the goats on his left. Then the King will say to those on his right hand, 'Come, you whom my Father has blessed, take for your heritage the kingdom prepared for you since the foundation of the world. For I was hungry and you gave me food; I was thirsty and you gave me drink; I was a stranger and you made me welcome; naked and you clothed me, sick and you visited me, in prison and you came to see me.' Then the virtuous will say to him in reply, 'Lord, when did we see you hungry and feed you; or thirsty and give you drink? When did we see you a stranger and make you welcome; naked and clothe you; sick or in prison and go to see you?' And the King will answer, 'I tell you solemnly, in so far as you did this to one of the least of these brothers of mine, you did it to me.' Next he will say to those on his left hand, 'Go away from me, with your curse upon you, to the eternal fire prepared for the devil and his angels. For I was hungry and you never gave me food; I was thirsty and you never gave me anything to drink; I was a stranger and you never made me welcome, naked and you never clothed me, sick and in prison and you never visited me. Then it will be their turn to ask, 'Lord, when did we see you hungry or thirsty, a stranger or naked, sick or in prison, and did not come to your help?' Then he will answer, 'I tell you solemnly, in so far as you neglected to do this to one of the least of these, you neglected to do it to me.' And they will go away to eternal punishment, and the virtuous to eternal life."

REFLECT

Our God does not sit idly by as we struggle through life, waiting to pass judgment on all our failings. True, judgment will come because God is fair, but Jesus Christ does all He can to prepare each of us ahead of time. In the first place, He came to earth; He became one of us, so that He could teach us using words and actions that we would understand. Second, He stays with us "until the end of time" (Matt. 28:20) through the ministry of His Church. The Church makes His teachings ring out in every age and place, constantly reminding us of the gospel's saving truths; through her, the Holy Spirit vivifies the sacraments in order to bring each of her children into intimate friendship with God; above all, through her, Christ stays literally at our side in the Eucharist, accompanying us patiently and lovingly in every tabernacle throughout the world. In this way, He hopes to make the Last Judgment a joyful reunion of intimate friends, not a surprise encounter between hostile strangers.

RESPOND

How could You have been clearer? You care about how I treat my neighbor, what I do for those around me. It seems so burdensome to live with my attention focused on others. I have so many needs, desires, and dreams of my own! But what matters most is not what I do, but who I am. Am I someone who loves, who gives, who serves? Self-giving is the one law of Heaven. If I can't learn to obey it now, I won't ever want to obey it later.

REST

In the end, You will make all things right. All the injustice and misery of the world will not escape Your goodness and Your power. I believe that You will come again, to judge, to rule, and to set things right. You wouldn't have promised this if You weren't planning on doing it. Help me to prepare for that day and to help everyone around me to prepare as well.

RESOLVE

How can I carry this encounter with me into the day? (Write / Journal)

CLOSING PRAYER OF THANKSGIVING

Turn to page 9

DAY 7
TUESDAY

PRAY LIKE A CHRISTIAN

"Mindful then of our condition, that we are essentially limited and absolutely dependent on the Supreme Being, before everything else let us have recourse to prayer. We know through faith how great is the power of humble, trustful, persevering prayer." ~POPE PIUS XI

READ: MATTHEW 6:7-15

"In your prayers do not babble as the pagans do, for they think that by using many words they will make themselves heard. Do not be like them; your Father knows what you need before you ask him. So you should pray like this: Our Father in heaven, may your name be held holy, your kingdom come, your will be done, on earth as in heaven. Give us today our daily bread. And forgive us our debts, as we have forgiven those who are in debt to us. And do not put us to the test, but save us from the evil one. Yes, if you forgive others their failings, your heavenly Father will forgive you yours; but if you do not forgive others, your Father will not forgive your failings either."

REFLECT

Friends share what they have with each other. Good friends freely share their most valuable possessions. By this standard, Christ's friendship is in a class all by itself. He didn't just share things, or knowledge, or companionship; He shared His nature as God's Son — His divine nature.

In this prayer, He teaches us to call God "Father." And to make sure we don't think that's just some pretty poetry, He also describes God as "your Father [who] knows what you need." In Christ, we have become not just citizens of God's Kingdom but members of God's family. We have Christ's blood flowing in our veins. We have an eternal inheritance; we have our own room in the heavenly mansion, our own family servant (our guardian angel), and the rest of the family is eagerly awaiting our arrival. This is the core message of the entire New Testament: through our incorporation into Christ and through our friendship with Him, we have become full members of God's household, along with everything that entails. Doesn't it make you want to pray the Our Father in an entirely new way?

RESPOND

Thank You for the gift of prayer. I can always raise my mind and heart to You, no matter where I am or what I'm doing. Thank You for the prayers and prayer commitments that You have brought into my life. I want to pray them well. I want to seek and find You in prayer, not just go through the motions. Stir my heart, Lord; remind me that You are my loving Father. Lord, teach me to pray.

REST

Thank You for Your priceless gift of forgiveness and for letting me experience that forgiveness so many times. I want to forgive as You forgive. You know who and what offends and hurts me most — and You permit those offenses and hurts. They give me opportunities to become more like You. Whom do I need to forgive right now? Have mercy on me, Lord, and make me merciful.

RESOLVE

How can I carry this encounter with me into the day? (Write / Journal)

CLOSING PRAYER OF THANKSGIVING

Turn to page 9

DAY 8
WEDNESDAY

THE MOST PRECIOUS SECRET

"Man has a noble task: that of prayer and
love. To pray and to love, that is the happiness
of man on earth." ~ST. JOHN VIANNEY

READ: LUKE 11:27–36

Now as he was speaking, a woman in the crowd raised her voice and said,
"Happy the womb that bore you and the breasts you sucked!" But he replied,
"Still happier those who hear the word of God and keep it!" The crowds
got even bigger and he addressed them, "This is a wicked generation; it is
asking for a sign. The only sign it will be given is the sign of Jonah. For just
as Jonah became a sign to the Ninevites, so will the Son of Man be to this
generation. On Judgement day the Queen of the South will rise up with the
men of this generation and condemn them, because she came from the ends
of the earth to hear the wisdom of Solomon; and there is something greater
than Solomon here. On Judgement day the men of Nineveh will stand up
with this generation and condemn it, because when Jonah preached they
repented; and there is something greater than Jonah here. No one lights a
lamp and puts it in some hidden place or under a tub, but on the lamp-stand
so that people may see the light when they come in. The lamp of your body
is your eye. When your eye is sound, your whole body too is filled with light;
but when it is diseased your body too will be all darkness. See to it then that
the light inside you is not darkness. If, therefore, your whole body is filled
with light, and no trace of darkness, it will be light entirely, as when the lamp
shines on you with its rays."

REFLECT

It must have warmed Christ's heart to hear the cheer this woman let loose in
the middle of His homily. She had detected His goodness and His beauty and
couldn't hold back her praise. What a contrast with the many self-righteous

intellectuals who sneered at the humble rabbi from Nazareth! But Jesus doesn't luxuriate in the compliment. He seizes the opportunity to reveal the secret that mankind had been seeking since before history began: what makes for a happy life. The human heart was made to find its true, lasting satisfaction only by living in communion with God, by knowing God and loving God — hearing and heeding God's word. The blessedness that comes from that outstrips even the most profound and worthy natural delights, such as that of being a parent to a great and wise rabbi. Jesus came to make that kind of happiness once again possible. Whoever trusts in Him, follows His teachings, and stays close to Him will experience it, just as the example of His closest friend of all time — His mother, Mary, whose moral and spiritual beauty He subtly complements in His response to the cheer — eloquently attests to.

RESPOND

When I take time to think about who You really are, Creator and Redeemer of all things, the infinite One, the all-powerful and all-loving and all-knowing God, I am filled with wonder. And to think that You want to walk with me, to guide my life. You suffered every kind of sorrow and humiliation in order to be able to prepare me a place in Your Kingdom. Blessed be Your name.

REST

The pace of life often carries me away, and I forget to keep You in my sight. I have to admit, the seductions of pleasure, wealth, popularity, power — they still attract me. Part of me still reaches out to those things. But my eye, the eye of my soul, recognizes that only You and Your will can give lasting meaning and fruitfulness. I want You, Lord. Teach me to do Your will.

RESOLVE

How can I carry this encounter with me into the day? (Write / Journal)

CLOSING PRAYER OF THANKSGIVING

Turn to page 9

DAY 9
THURSDAY

IMAGINING GOD'S GOODNESS

"Teach me to seek you, and reveal yourself to me as I seek, because I can neither seek you if you do not teach me how, nor find you unless you reveal yourself." ~ST. ANSELM

READ: MATTHEW 7:7-14

"Ask, and it will be given to you; search, and you will find; knock, and the door will be opened to you. For the one who asks always receives; the one who searches always finds; the one who knocks will always have the door opened to him. Is there a man among you who would hand his son a stone when he asked for bread? Or would hand him a snake when he asked for a fish? If you, then, who are evil, know how to give your children what is good, how much more will your Father in heaven give good things to those who ask him! So always treat others as you would like them to treat you; that is the meaning of the Law and the Prophets. Enter by the narrow gate, since the road that leads to perdition is wide and spacious, and many take it; but it is a narrow gate and a hard road that leads to life, and only a few find it."

REFLECT

Friendship cannot be forced, not even friendship with God. Since Christ wants us to relate to Him as friends, not as zombies, He refuses to force us to follow Him. He lets us seek happiness in the world's many empty wells and false promises, if we so choose. And yet He wants us to look for it in Him. Imagine how eagerly and energetically He pronounced this threefold command: "Ask! Seek! Knock!" It's as if He is pleading for us to turn to Him, to let Him be our guide and coach and Savior and friend. It's all His heart wants. Why do so many refuse the invitation?

RESPOND

Certain things always remind me of Your goodness: the beauties of nature, the crucifix, the love of my family.... How many there are! Right now I want to contemplate them, to remember them.... Strengthen my conviction, Lord, that You are the perfect Father, who loves me even more than I love myself. Always remind me of Your goodness, so I will never, ever walk away from You.

REST

I believe in You, Lord, and so I believe You when You say that the meaning of life and the quality of my discipleship correspond to the way I treat my neighbor in thought, word, and deed. And isn't that how You lived? Your whole life was one continuous act of self-giving that reached its climax on the Cross. Teach me to give my whole self to You. Jesus, meek and humble of heart, make my heart more like Yours.

Whenever I have really asked, sought, or knocked, You have rewarded me with a new experience of Your goodness. Why don't I ask more? Is it because I think I can give meaning and fruitfulness to my life all by myself? That is foolish, I know. But I am a fool, Lord. I need Your wisdom and grace to transform me.

RESOLVE

How can I carry this encounter with me into the day? (Write / Journal)

CLOSING PRAYER OF THANKSGIVING

Turn to page 9

DAY 10
FRIDAY

THE HEART OF THE MATTER

"The Christian life is the continuation and completion of the life of Christ in us. We should be so many Christs here on earth, continuing his life and his works, laboring and suffering." ~ST. JOHN EUDES

READ: MATTHEW 5:20 37

"For I tell you, if your virtue goes no deeper than that of the scribes and Pharisees, you will never get into the kingdom of heaven. You have learnt how it was said to our ancestors: You must not kill; and if anyone does kill he must answer for it before the court. But I say this to you: anyone who is angry with his brother will answer for it before the court; if a man calls his brother Fool he will answer for it before the Sanhedrin; and if a man calls him Renegade he will answer for it in hell fire. So then, if you are bringing your offering to the altar and there remember that your brother has something against you, leave your offering there before the altar, go and be reconciled with your brother first, and then come back and present your offering. Come to terms with your opponent in good time while you are still on the way to the court with him, or he may hand you over to the judge and the judge to the officer, and you will be thrown into prison. I tell you solemnly, you will not get out till you have paid the last penny.

"You have learnt how it was said: You must not commit adultery. But I say this to you: if a man looks at a woman lustfully, he has already committed adultery with her in his heart. If your right eye should cause you to sin, tear it out and throw it away; for it will do you less harm to lose one part of you than to have your whole body thrown into hell. And if your right hand should cause you to sin, cut it off and throw it away; for it will do you less harm to lose one part of you than to have your whole body go to hell. It has also been said: Anyone who divorces his wife must give her a writ of dismissal. But I say this to you: everyone who divorces his wife, except for the case of fornication, makes her an adulteress; and anyone who marries a divorced woman commits adultery.

"Again, you have learnt how it was said to our ancestors: You must not break your oath, but must fulfill your oaths to the Lord. But I say this to you: do not swear at all, either by heaven, since that is God's throne; or by the earth, since that is his footstool; or by Jerusalem, since that is the city of the great king. Do not swear by your own head either, since you cannot turn a single hair white or black. All you need say is Yes if you mean yes, No if you mean no; anything more than this comes from the evil one."

REFLECT

The Greek word Jesus uses for "Hell" is *Gehenna*. Gehenna was Jerusalem's garbage dump. It had been the valley where unfaithful Jews in past centuries offered human sacrifices to foreign gods. When the nation reformed and such practices were stopped, they decided to use Gehenna as an open-air incinerator. Thus, the ever-smoldering, worm-infested valley became a symbol for the place where people who reject friendship with God suffer eternal frustration: Hell.

Christ's frequent mention of Hell in the Gospels has caused some critics to accuse Christianity of manipulating weak and superstitious people by instilling fear. Nothing could be less accurate. Christ's warnings are those of a friend. If you were in a car with a friend and saw that he was about to collide with an oncoming eighteen-wheeler, you would try to get him to turn out of the way. Jesus knows that we can reach lasting happiness only through friendship with God, and He wants us to be happy, so He warns us about everything that could damage or destroy that friendship. The truth is that eternity spent without God will be indescribably painful because the human person was created to live in union with God. Since Christ loves us, He tells us the truth — even the tough truth.

RESPOND

You care about what happens in my mind and my heart — where only You and I can see. Help me to look there now; show me what is pleasing to You and what is not, and then change what is not. Please, Lord — You know I can't do it on my own. You know how self-centered and wounded I am. If You don't change my heart, it will never change. Jesus, meek and humble of heart, make my heart more like Yours.

REST

Why do You give so much importance to such little things? A false promise here, a lustful fantasy there, an angry or spiteful word now and then ... Lord, why don't You teach us about political systems and economic justice — the big picture? Somehow, the little picture of each soul matters more to You. Make me wise, Lord; teach me to follow You.

Some aspects of Your will are harder for me to follow than others. Some of the Church's teachings I understand easily — others not so much. It doesn't matter, Lord. What matters is that I know it comes from You, my Creator and Redeemer. I want to do Your will, no matter how hard. Increase my weak faith; Jesus, I trust in You.

RESOLVE

How can I carry this encounter with me into the day? (Write / Journal)

CLOSING PRAYER OF THANKSGIVING

Turn to page 9

GIVING LIKE GOD

"Finally, may Christ inflame the desires of all men to break through the barriers which divide them, to strengthen the bonds of mutual love, to learn to understand one another, and to pardon those who have done them wrong." ~POPE JOHN XXIII

READ: MATTHEW 5:38-48

"You have learnt how it was said: Eye for eye and tooth for tooth. But I say this to you: offer the wicked man no resistance. On the contrary, if anyone hits you on the right cheek, offer him the other as well; if a man takes you to law and would have your tunic, let him have your cloak as well. And if anyone orders you to go one mile, go two miles with him. Give to anyone who asks, and if anyone wants to borrow, do not turn away. You have learnt how it was said: You must love your neighbor and hate your enemy. But I say this to you: love your enemies and pray for those who persecute you; in this way, you will be sons of your Father in heaven, for he causes his sun to rise on bad men as well as good, and his rain to fall on honest and dishonest men alike. For if you love those who love you, what right have you to claim any credit? Even the tax collectors do as much, do they not? And if you save your greetings for your brothers, are you doing anything exceptional? Even the pagans do as much, do they not? You must therefore be perfect just as your heavenly Father is perfect."

REFLECT

God makes the sun shine and the rain fall on both His faithful children and the rebellious ones. His love is, in the truest sense of the word, unconditional. This means that the friendship He offers us in Christ is also unconditional. Christ is the true friend, whose love and devotion to you doesn't depend on looks, popularity, intelligence, success, money, or anything else: He loves you simply because you are you. He can't love you any more than He already does. There is no pressure here, only peace.

A lot of good it would do if Christ gave these impossible instructions (to love as He loves) and then left us alone to try to carry them out. But He doesn't. He walks this narrow and steep path in front of us and beside us. That was the lesson of Good Friday, when He was betrayed and abandoned by His closest friends, cruelly tortured, slandered, publicly humiliated, unjustly condemned, and put to death. Throughout the ordeal, He never once resented, hated, or retaliated. The love in His heart and His trust in the Father buoyed Him up, to the point where His dying words included, "Father, forgive them, they know not what they do" (Luke 23:34, NABRE). That also is the lesson of the Eucharist, the supernatural food of our Christian souls; Christ gives it to us to supplement our weak efforts and to keep us strong as we follow His difficult path.

RESPOND

Sometimes, Lord (and You know which times I'm talking about), it's hard for me to turn the other cheek, hand over my cloak, and go the extra mile. It is not natural to love one's enemies, Lord, so if You want me to do this, I am going to need a lot of help. But I want to. I know that only truly Christian love will bring peace to my heart and to the world. Lord Jesus, give me strength.

You have forgiven me so many times. You have practiced everything You preached in relation to me. Somehow, You really do love me. You really are interested in my life. How can that be? I don't understand, but I believe, and I thank You with all my heart, Lord — You know how much I need Your love. Teach me to love as You do.

REST

There are so many things I want to do for You and Your Church, Lord. My mind and heart are full of desires to change this world and bring everyone around me into Your friendship. Yet I can barely control my own temper. Help me to focus on the most important thing: loving my neighbor as You have loved me.

RESOLVE

How can I carry this encounter with me into the day? (Write / Journal)

CLOSING PRAYER OF THANKSGIVING

Turn to page 9

DAY 12
SECOND SUNDAY OF LENT

MOUNTAINTOP MEETINGS

"If he were not of the same nature as ourselves,
his command to imitate him as a master
would be a futile one." ~ST. HIPPOLYTUS

READ: MATTHEW 17:1-13

Six days later, Jesus took with him Peter and James and his brother John and led them up a high mountain where they could be alone. There in their presence he was transfigured: his face shone like the sun and his clothes became as white as the light. Suddenly Moses and Elijah appeared to them; they were talking with him. Then Peter spoke to Jesus. "Lord," he said, "it is wonderful for us to be here; if you wish, I will make three tents here, one for you, one for Moses and one for Elijah." He was still speaking when suddenly a bright cloud covered them with shadow, and from the cloud there came a voice which said, "This is my Son, the Beloved; he enjoys my favor. Listen to him." When they heard this the disciples fell on their faces overcome with fear. But Jesus came up and touched them. "Stand up," he said, "do not be afraid." And when they raised their eyes they saw no one but only Jesus. As they came down from the mountain Jesus gave them this order, "Tell no one about the vision until the Son of Man has risen from the dead." And the disciples put this question to him, "Why do the scribes say then that Elijah has to come first?" "True," he replied, "Elijah is to come to see that everything is once more as it should be; however, I tell you that Elijah has come already and they did not recognise him but treated him as they pleased; and the Son of Man will suffer similarly at their hands." The disciples understood then that he had been speaking of John the Baptist.

REFLECT

The Church has always recognized the Transfiguration as a theophany, a visible manifestation of God. Christ Himself is the Second Person of the

Trinity; the cloud represents the Holy Spirit, the Third Person (who hovered over the waters before creation: see Gen. 1:2); and the voice is of God the Father, the First Person, speaking as plainly as we could ever ask for, in order to teach us the one necessary lesson: "Listen to him [Christ]." It is the same lesson that came at the theophany during Jesus' baptism at the hands of John the Baptist, the new Elijah, who was to usher in the age of the Messiah. In St. Matthew's Gospel, God the Father speaks only twice from Heaven, and He says essentially the same thing both times. It behooves us to consider deeply what that saying means.

Listening to Christ means getting to know Him, understanding His heart, and heeding His call in our lives. Jesus Christ is God's own Son, sent by the Father to be our guide to fulfillment, to the meaning and happiness we all long for. There is "no other name under heaven given among men by which we must be saved" (Acts 4:12). Christ alone is the answer, the secret to a life lived to the full. All we need to do is listen to Him, to turn our gaze to Him. How? By spending time in heartfelt prayer, by delving into the marvelous teachings of the Church, by steeping ourselves in the priceless living waters of the Gospels and the rest of Holy Scripture, by experiencing Christ Himself truly present in the Eucharist, and most of all by doing His will each day with faith, hope, and love, no matter what the cost.

RESPOND

You are the Lord of life and history. I believe in You, Lord. I believe that You are the focal point of all human history. I put my life in Your hands. I want to serve You, to walk with You, to help build Your kingdom. I want to follow You, Lord, today, tomorrow, and every day of my life, no matter what You may ask of me.

Sometimes I wish that You would show Yourself to me as marvelously as You did to these three apostles. Wouldn't that make it easier to follow You? But You know exactly what I need. All of Your life, Your doctrine, and Your love are mine. I have the Gospels, the Church, the Eucharist, my spirituality. I have Your forgiveness, guaranteed. Lord, the time has come for me to stop complaining. Christ, be my life.

REST

The cross still frightens me. I want things to go smoothly; I want to stay on the mountaintop. But You didn't stay there. How much rejection, envy, and betrayal You suffered! And You did it to teach me what love really is:

self-giving and self-forgetting. You love me with a personal, determined love. Teach me to love like that, with fidelity in tough times, with sincere deeds, no matter what the cost. Jesus, I trust in You.

RESOLVE
How can I carry this encounter with me into the day? (Write / Journal)

CLOSING PRAYER OF THANKSGIVING
Turn to page 9

DAY 13
MONDAY

LOVE, GIVE, AND LIVE

"The measure of love is to love without measure." ~ST. AUGUSTINE

READ: LUKE 6:27-38

"But I say this to you who are listening: Love your enemies, do good to those who hate you, bless those who curse you, pray for those who treat you badly. To the man who slaps you on one cheek, present the other cheek too; to the man who takes your cloak from you, do not refuse your tunic. Give to everyone who asks you, and do not ask for your property back from the man who robs you. Treat others as you would like them to treat you. If you love those who love you, what thanks can you expect? Even sinners love those who love them. And if you do good to those who do good to you, what thanks can you expect? For even sinners do that much. And if you lend to those from whom you hope to receive, what thanks can you expect? Even sinners lend to sinners to get back the same amount. Instead, love your enemies and do good, and lend without any hope of return. You will have a great reward, and you will be sons of the Most High, for he himself is kind to the ungrateful and the wicked. Be compassionate as your Father is compassionate. Do not judge, and you will not be judged yourselves; do not condemn, and you will not be condemned yourselves; grant pardon, and you will be pardoned. Give, and there will be gifts for you: a full measure, pressed down, shaken together, and running over, will be poured into your lap; because the amount you measure out is the amount you will be given back."

REFLECT

Jesus presents us with a new way of living so that our "reward will be great" and there will be gifts for us. Sometimes we mistakenly think that a Christian ought somehow to be indifferent to the human desire for happiness, as if wanting to be happy were some kind of sin. The truth is much more realistic:

the desire for happiness is a gift from God, a homing device that impels us toward God, the only source of true and lasting happiness. If Christ demands sacrifice and generosity, if his way of life seems hard, if the cross is painful, it's only a temporary pain, like that of someone recovering from reconstructive surgery: the doctor demands a long and arduous rehabilitation program so that the patient can once again enjoy a healthy, active, and happy life. Christ is the doctor of our fallen, selfish souls, and He eagerly looks forward to the day when we will join Him on the tennis courts in Heaven.

RESPOND

You want me to be truly happy. You will never be satisfied for me to settle for the counterfeit happiness this world offers, the kind I sometimes would prefer. You love me too much. I believe in You, Lord, but it's hard to follow Your path. I need Your grace. You know I do. You will never hoard Your help. Thank You, Lord. Teach me to do Your will.

REST

Your standard of love is much too high for me. So if You want me to live that way, You are going to have to come and be my light and my strength. Send Your Holy Spirit into my soul and into the souls of all the members of Your Church. Grant us a renewal of authentic Christian charity. You are all-powerful, Lord — You can do it! Come, Holy Spirit, enkindle in me the fire of Your love.

RESOLVE

How can I carry this encounter with me into the day? (Write / Journal)

CLOSING PRAYER OF THANKSGIVING

Turn to page 9

DAY 14
TUESDAY

LEARNING FROM THE PHARISEES

"The man who loves God thinks it enough to please him whom he loves, for no greater reward can be sought than that love itself." ~POPE ST. LEO THE GREAT

READ: MATTHEW 23:1-12

Then addressing the people and his disciples Jesus said, "The scribes and the Pharisees occupy the chair of Moses. You must therefore do what they tell you and listen to what they say; but do not be guided by what they do: since they do not practice what they preach. They tie up heavy burdens and lay them on men's shoulders, but will they lift a finger to move them? Not they! Everything they do is done to attract attention, like wearing broader phylacteries and longer tassels, like wanting to take the place of honor at banquets and the front seats in the synagogues, being greeted obsequiously in the market squares and having people call them Rabbi. You, however, must not allow yourselves to be called Rabbi, since you have only one master, and you are all brothers. You must call no one on earth your father, since you have only one Father, and he is in heaven. Nor must you allow yourselves to be called teachers, for you have only one Teacher, the Christ. The greatest among you must be your servant. Anyone who exalts himself will be humbled, and anyone who humbles himself will be exalted."

REFLECT

It must have been difficult for Jesus to speak so harshly about the Pharisees and the scribes. He did so only for the sake of the crowds and the disciples who had witnessed the ongoing controversy. Jesus has done everything in His power — while still respecting his enemies' freedom — to win over His attackers, to meet them on their own ground, to open their closed minds to His saving truth. Only then does he pronounce judgment on them. Even this harsh task of uprooting the Jewish authorities — a task Jesus has the right and duty to perform, for the sake of those whom the authorities were leading astray — is performed with generosity, in the context of teaching a lesson that will serve the good of all.

Christ taught this lesson many times with words, all the time with His actions, and one time forever with His Passion, the ultimate expression of His love: "He emptied himself, taking the form of a slave, coming in human likeness; and found human in appearance, he humbled himself, becoming obedient to death, even death on a cross" (Phil. 2:7–8, NABRE).

RESPOND

Never let me deceive myself, Lord. Help me to see myself as I truly am. I want to follow You, to hear Your voice each moment, to see Your providential, loving action in every happening and encounter of my life. Teach me to walk by faith, Lord, not by sight.

REST

I can strive to please You only if I know what truly pleases You. And I can know what pleases You only if I study and pray. I need You to keep me humble, Lord. I tend so easily to slip into that self-destructive thirst for recognition and superiority. That tendency goes deep — only Your love goes deeper. Purify my heart, Lord. Teach me to think first of others and then of myself, just as You did. Jesus, I trust in You.

RESOLVE

How can I carry this encounter with me into the day? (Write / Journal)

CLOSING PRAYER OF THANKSGIVING

Turn to page 9

DAY 15
WEDNESDAY

SERVANTS AND SIGNS

"He it is whose sufferings are shared by the martyrs with their glorious courage and by all those who believe and are born again at the moment of their regeneration." ~POPE ST. LEO THE GREAT

READ: MATTHEW 20:20–34

Then the mother of Zebedee's sons came with her sons to make a request of him, and bowed low; and he said to her, "What is it you want?" She said to him, "Promise that these two sons of mine may sit one at your right hand and the other at your left in your kingdom." "You do not know what you are asking," Jesus answered. "Can you drink the cup that I am going to drink?" They replied, "We can." "Very well," he said, "you shall drink my cup, but as for seats at my right hand and my left, these are not mine to grant; they belong to those to whom they have been allotted by my Father." When the other ten heard this they were indignant with the two brothers. But Jesus called them to him and said, "You know that among the pagans the rulers lord it over them, and their great men make their authority felt. This is not to happen among you. No; anyone who wants to be great among you must be your servant, and anyone who wants to be first among you must be your slave, just as the Son of Man came not to be served but to serve, and to give his life as a ransom for many."

As they left Jericho a large crowd followed him. Now there were two blind men sitting at the side of the road. When they heard that it was Jesus who was passing by, they shouted, "Lord! Have pity on us, Son of David." And the crowd scolded them and told them to keep quiet, but they only shouted more loudly, "Lord! Have pity on us, Son of David." Jesus stopped, called them over and said, "What do you want me to do for you?" They said to him, "Lord, let us have our sight back." Jesus felt pity for them and touched their eyes, and immediately their sight returned and they followed him.

REFLECT

James and John send their mother to make a bold request, one they were probably ashamed to make themselves (as evidenced by the umbrage the other disciples take at hearing about it). Jesus sees through their ploy. He addresses His answer to James and John and not to their mother. But He answers without taking offense. He is glad that these two disciples want to be close to Him and be great in His Kingdom. If He could give them what they have asked for, He would. But since He can't promise them that, He will give them the next best thing: they, too, will suffer for the Kingdom (thus staying close to Him). Here He teaches them the secret to real greatness — serving, giving, forgetting oneself. Is our path any different? Jesus wants us to confide in Him, to be honest with Him; that's all He needs in order to make us His everlasting friends.

RESPOND

I, too, want to see, Lord. I want to see You. I want to see the truth about myself, about the world, and about the meaning of life. I want to see Your will for me and the way to fulfill it. I want to see the needs of those around me and how to meet them. I want to see the beauty of Your doctrine and of Your heart, so that no other ambition will interfere with my striving to be truly great in Your Kingdom.

REST

Lord, I am reluctant to serve. My natural tendency is to want to be served, especially at home, among those I should serve most. So often I think first of myself. But if You call me to follow in Your footsteps, to give my life for others, then it must be possible. You never ask the impossible. Through You, with You, and in You, I can be all that You created me to be. Okay, Lord, whatever You want. Thy will be done.

RESOLVE

How can I carry this encounter with me into the day? (Write / Journal)

CLOSING PRAYER OF THANKSGIVING

Turn to page 9

DAY 16
THURSDAY

MONEY AND FIRE

"Girding our loins then with faith and the observance of good deeds let us so follow his paths under the guidance of the gospel that we may be worthy to see him who has called us into his kingdom." ~ST. BENEDICT, RULE, PROLOGUE

READ: LUKE 16:19-31

"There was a rich man who used to dress in purple and fine linen and feast magnificently every day. And at his gate there lay a poor man called Lazarus, covered with sores, who longed to fill himself with the scraps that fell from the rich man's table. Dogs even came and licked his sores. Now the poor man died and was carried away by the angels to the bosom of Abraham. The rich man also died and was buried. In his torment in Hades he looked up and saw Abraham a long way off with Lazarus in his bosom. So he cried out, 'Father Abraham, pity me and send Lazarus to dip the tip of his finger in water and cool my tongue, for I am in agony in these flames.' 'My son,' Abraham replied, 'remember that during your life good things came your way, just as bad things came the way of Lazarus. Now he is being comforted here while you are in agony. But that is not all: between us and you a great gulf has been fixed, to stop anyone, if he wanted to, crossing from our side to yours, and to stop any crossing from your side to ours.' The rich man replied, 'Father, I beg you then to send Lazarus to my father's house, since I have five brothers, to give them warning so that they do not come to this place of torment too.' 'They have Moses and the prophets,' said Abraham, 'let them listen to them.' 'Ah no, father Abraham,' said the rich man, 'but if someone comes to them from the dead, they will repent.' Then Abraham said to him, 'If they will not listen either to Moses or to the prophets, they will not be convinced even if someone should rise from the dead.'"

REFLECT

Perhaps Christ's greatest act of charity was His patient effort to win over the hearts of the self-satisfied Pharisees. Many of them showed no sign of respect or even mild interest in the truth of His claims, and yet He kept buffeting them with parables and miracles, desperately hoping that they would let in the light of His grace. Christ commanded His disciples to love their enemies, to forgive those who persecuted them, and He shows them how — by being a true friend to His most vicious antagonists.

He continues this conquest of love. Yesterday, today, and tomorrow, Jesus continues to go after every single soul. He wants to hold each one close to His heart, just as Lazarus was held close in Abraham's bosom. It is God's will that none be lost. His mission is to draw all men to Himself. This is the desire in the heart of our Friend, and if we are to be faithful, it should become our desire too, for He has given us a share in this same mission of gathering souls to the bosom of the Father.

RESPOND

So many people live as if this life were all there is. Why? Why don't we believe in Heaven and Hell? I admit, it's possible to get obsessed with the afterlife, but it would be a foolish traveler who kept moving ahead every day without ever thinking about his destination. Keep me in tune with the truth, Lord, and teach me to bear witness with courage and love.

REST

Who are my enemies, my antagonists? Do I love them as You loved Yours? The Pharisees didn't give You warm, fuzzy feelings, but You loved them all the same. You went out of Your way to give them what they most needed — a vision of Your love and truth. Teach me to love as You love and to give as You give.

RESOLVE

How can I carry this encounter with me into the day? (Write / Journal)

CLOSING PRAYER OF THANKSGIVING

Turn to page 9

DAY 17
FRIDAY

A VALUABLE VINEYARD

"My daughter, all your miseries have been consumed in the flame of My love, like a little twig thrown into a roaring fire." ~JESUS TO ST. FAUSTINA KOWALSKA

READ: MATTHEW 21:33–46

"Listen to another parable. There was a man, a landowner, who planted a vineyard; he fenced it round, dug a winepress in it and built a tower; then he leased it to tenants and went abroad. When vintage time drew near he sent his servants to the tenants to collect his produce. But the tenants seized his servants, thrashed one, killed another and stoned a third. Next he sent some more servants, this time a larger number, and they dealt with them in the same way. Finally, he sent his son to them. 'They will respect my son,' he said. But when the tenants saw the son, they said to each other, 'This is the heir. Come on, let us kill him and take over his inheritance.' So they seized him and threw him out of the vineyard and killed him. Now when the owner of the vineyard comes, what will he do to those tenants?" They answered, "He will bring those wretches to a wretched end and lease the vineyard to other tenants who will deliver the produce to him when the season arrives." Jesus said to them, "Have you never read in the scriptures: 'It was the stone rejected by the builders that became the keystone. This was the Lord's doing and it is wonderful to see'? I tell you, then, that the kingdom of God will be taken from you and given to a people who will produce its fruit." When they heard his parables, the chief priests and the scribes realized he was speaking about them, but though they would have liked to arrest him they were afraid of the crowds, who looked on him as a prophet.

REFLECT

The owner of the vineyard would have had every right to punish the tenants after they had done away with the first batch of servants. But he didn't. He sent more and more, and finally he sent his son. Only when we have made a definitive decision against Christ and held fast to that decision in the face of abundant gestures of His love will He let us have what we have wrongly chosen. Christ, the true friend, does not condemn those who refuse His friendship; they condemn themselves.

Jesus: I will never give up on you. If only you knew how much I love my Church and every person in it. If only you knew how patient my Father is, how magnificently and unabashedly He loves each one of His children! Since I will never give up on you, you must never give up on yourself. No matter how many times you offend me, fail, or reject me, I am always ready and willing to renew our friendship. I am always taking the first step, moving you and inspiring you to come back to me.

RESPOND

I pray for those who are far from You, for those who don't recognize the hardness of their own hearts. Conquer them with Your grace. Don't let them perish but grant them eternal life. All things are possible for You, Lord, so soften their hearts. Reach out to them through me. I, too, want to give my life for the salvation of others. For the sake of Your sorrowful Passion, have mercy on us and on the whole world.

What are You saying to me that I am not hearing? What relationship do I need to reform? What responsibility am I neglecting? What mission am I ignoring? Lord, I know that following You will always require the painful steps of humility. Never let me take any other path. Never let me be separated from You.

REST

Thank You for never giving up on me. Thank You for being so patient with me. Thank You for inspiring good desires in my heart. Lord, teach me to be truly humble, to place all my confidence in You, and to learn the secret of lasting joy. Make me a channel of Your peace.

RESOLVE

How can I carry this encounter with me into the day? (Write / Journal)

CLOSING PRAYER OF THANKSGIVING

Turn to page 9

DAY 18
SATURDAY

COMING HOME

"On the basis of this way of manifesting the presence of God who is Father, love, and mercy, Jesus makes mercy one of the principal themes of his preaching." ~ST. JOHN PAUL II

READ: LUKE 15:11-32

He also said, "A man had two sons. The younger said to his father, 'Father, let me have the share of the estate that would come to me.' So the father divided the property between them. A few days later, the younger son got together everything he had and left for a distant country where he squandered his money on a life of debauchery. When he had spent it all, that country experienced a severe famine, and now he began to feel the pinch, so he hired himself out to one of the local inhabitants who put him on his farm to feed the pigs. And he would willingly have filled his belly with the husks the pigs were eating but no one offered him anything. Then he came to his senses and said, 'How many of my father's paid servants have more food than they want, and here am I dying of hunger! I will leave this place and go to my father and say: Father, I have sinned against heaven and against you; I no longer deserve to be called your son; treat me as one of your paid servants.' So he left the place and went back to his father. While he was still a long way off, his father saw him and was moved with pity. He ran to the boy, clasped him in his arms and kissed him tenderly. Then his son said, 'Father, I have sinned against heaven and against you. I no longer deserve to be called your son.' But the father said to his servants, 'Quick! Bring out the best robe and put it on him; put a ring on his finger and sandals on his feet. Bring the calf we have been fattening, and kill it; we are going to have a feast, a celebration, because this son of mine was dead and has come back to life; he was lost and is found.' And they began to celebrate.

"Now the elder son was out in the fields, and on his way back, as he drew near the house, he could hear music and dancing. Calling one of the servants he asked what it was all about. 'Your brother has come,' replied the servant, 'and your father has killed the calf we had fattened because he has got him back safe and sound.' He was angry then and refused to go in, and his father came out to plead with him; but he answered his father, 'Look, all these years I have slaved for you and never once disobeyed your orders, yet you never offered me so much as a kid for me to celebrate with my friends. But, for this son of yours, when he comes back after swallowing up your property — he and his women — you kill the calf we had been fattening.' The father said, 'My son, you are with me always and all I have is yours. But it was only right we should celebrate and rejoice, because your brother here was dead and has come to life; he was lost and is found.' "

REFLECT

Many leaders in the world are "in it for themselves." Christ isn't. His greatest glory is winning people's hearts for God, which also happens to be the best thing for them. When the Pharisees complained about His generosity to sinners, He made the most of their attention to try to teach them a lesson. He didn't have to — they certainly didn't deserve His mercy — but He chose to. Then, in the parable itself, Christ profiles His own heart — the heart of God — in the behavior of the father, who lived only for his sons' well-being. "All I have is yours" is no empty rhetoric: in Christ, in the Church, in the Eucharist, God has held absolutely nothing back from us. Jesus is Lord, but He is the Lord of love, longing for hearts that will submit to His gentle and life-giving reign.

RESPOND

Whereas the Pharisees needed to understand Your goodness and mercy, I think that at times I need to be more aware of the evil of sin. I have been infected by the prevailing mentality that forgets about personal responsibility and about the wounds that selfishness causes to others. Lord, why do I act as if self-centeredness were okay? Free me, Lord, to love.

Something made that younger son come back to his senses. You are working in mysterious, hidden ways in every heart. I have placed my hope in You because I believe that You are the way, the truth, and the life. But sometimes I have less confidence in Your ability to help others who seem so far from the truth to come to their senses. Increase my hope, Lord.

REST

I don't have to go far to find people who are in trouble, who are sad, who need to come back to You and don't know the way. Open my heart so I can reach out to them. Will You not use my slightest effort, even if it's clumsy, as a channel of grace? I don't want to hoard the treasure You have given me — knowing Your love. The more I give away, the more You will give to me.

RESOLVE

How can I carry this encounter with me into the day? (Write / Journal)

CLOSING PRAYER OF THANKSGIVING

Turn to page 9

DAY 19
THIRD SUNDAY OF LENT

QUENCHING CHRIST'S THIRST

*"To show that he was not different from us, he
undertook hard work, he went hungry and thirsty,
he took rest and sleep, he did not shirk suffering,
he revealed the Resurrection." ~ST. HIPPOLYTUS*

READ: JOHN 4:5-26

He came to the Samaritan town called Sychar, near the land that Jacob gave to his son Joseph. Jacob's well is there and Jesus, tired by the journey, sat straight down by the well. It was about the sixth hour. When a Samaritan woman came to draw water, Jesus said to her, "Give me a drink." His disciples had gone into the town to buy food. The Samaritan woman said to him, "What? You are a Jew and you ask me, a Samaritan, for a drink?" — Jews, in fact, do not associate with Samaritans. Jesus replied: "If you only knew what God is offering and who it is that is saying to you: Give me a drink, you would have been the one to ask, and he would have given you living water." "You have no bucket, sir," she answered, "and the well is deep: how could you get this living water? Are you a greater man than our father Jacob who gave us this well and drank from it himself with his sons and his cattle?" Jesus replied: "Whoever drinks this water will get thirsty again; but anyone who drinks the water that I shall give will never be thirsty again: the water that I shall give will turn into a spring inside him, welling up to eternal life."

"Sir," said the woman, "give me some of that water, so that I may never get thirsty and never have to come here again to draw water." "Go and call your husband," said Jesus to her, "and come back here." The woman answered, "I have no husband." He said to her, "You are right to say, 'I have no husband'; for although you have had five, the one you have now is not your husband. You spoke the truth there." "I see you are a prophet, sir," said the woman. "Our fathers worshipped on this mountain, while you say that Jerusalem is the place where one ought to worship." Jesus said: "Believe me, woman, the hour is coming when you will worship the Father neither on this mountain nor in Jerusalem. You worship what you do not know; we worship what we do know: for salvation comes from the Jews. But the hour will come — in fact it is here already — when true worshippers will worship the Father in spirit and truth: that is the kind of worshipper the Father wants. God is spirit, and those who worship must worship in spirit and truth." The woman said to him, "I know that Messiah — that is, Christ — is coming; and when he comes he will tell us everything." "I who am speaking to you," said Jesus, "I am he."

REFLECT

The Samaritan woman: I knew something was different about that man as soon as I came up to the well. He looked at me in a way that men didn't usually look at me. I met His eyes for just a second, and then I looked away. But I wanted to look again. I had seen in His glance something that I had only dreamed about before: He knew me completely — He knew exactly what kind of person I was. Yet it didn't bother Him; in fact, it was as if He was glad to see me — not because He wanted anything from me but because He seemed to want something for me, as if He were pure kindness. So when I looked away — because that was the proper thing to do — I was just dying to look at Him again, to see that kindness in His eyes, to drink it in.

But then I thought, no, it's only my imagination. And then He spoke to me. He asked me for a drink. And that was the beginning of a conversation that changed my life. I didn't understand everything He told me, but I understood that He knew me — He knew me through and through, and He still cared about me; He was interested in me. To Him, I was important, not just because I could give Him something but just ... well, just because. In His eyes, I mattered. Even then I knew that what He said about being the Messiah was true. How else could I explain the change that was already happening in my heart? It was as if a door had opened in my life where before there had been only a thick, dark, high wall protecting my broken heart. He freed me. I had to tell the others in the town. I knew He was the Savior, and I just had to tell everyone. I knew that as soon as they met Him they, too, would realize it. And they did! Before that day, I was just surviving; after that encounter with His words, His glance, His presence — from then on, I began to live.

RESPOND

Jesus, tell me everything. Tell me about myself and the meaning of my life; tell me about Your love and Your wisdom and Your plan for my life. Lord, give me Your living water — how thirsty I am! I have tasted Your gifts; I know at least a little bit about what You are offering. I want to know more. I want to live closer to You. I want to lead others to Your heart, just as you led me. I believe in You, Lord, and in Your eagerness to save souls who are stuck in sin and darkness. And I believe that You can save them, just as you turned this woman's life around — just as you have turned my life around. Thank You for guiding me. Thank You for not giving up on me. Thank You for giving me a mission in life.

REST

What does it mean, Lord, to worship in "spirit and truth"? You want it; You came to make it possible. To worship is to acknowledge Your greatness, majesty, and goodness. You want me to do so not only in external ceremonies but in my heart, in my attitudes, in my choices. You want me to live as You would have me live, Lord, trusting in You, seeking Your will always. Teach me to do so, because this is what You desire.

RESOLVE

How can I carry this encounter with me into the day? (Write / Journal)

CLOSING PRAYER OF THANKSGIVING

Turn to page 9

TROUBLES AT HOME

"If you search for the reason why a man loves God, you will find no other reason at all, save that God first loved him." ~ST. AUGUSTINE

READ: LUKE 4:22–30

And he won the approval of all, and they were astonished by the gracious words that came from his lips. They said, "This is Joseph's son, surely?" But he replied, "No doubt you will quote me the saying, 'Physician, heal yourself' and tell me, 'We have heard all that happened in Capernaum, do the same here in your own countryside.'" And he went on, "I tell you solemnly, no prophet is ever accepted in his own country. There were many widows in Israel, I can assure you, in Elijah's day, when heaven remained shut for three years and six months and a great famine raged throughout the land, but Elijah was not sent to any one of these: he was sent to a widow at Zarephath, a Sidonian town. And in the prophet Elisha's time there were many lepers in Israel, but none of these was cured, except the Syrian, Naaman." When they heard this everyone in the synagogue was enraged. They sprang to their feet and hustled him out of the town; and they took him up to the brow of the hill their town was built on, intending to throw him down the cliff, but he slipped through the crowd and walked away.

REFLECT

John: I often wondered why Jesus didn't claim His rights. He could have — there were many times when I wanted Him to. If He had stayed more aloof in public, perhaps more people would have believed in Him — people are funny that way. If He had insulated Himself behind hundreds of servants and deputies and courtiers, letting Himself be seen and heard only on the rarest of occasions and performing an impressive miracle every once in a while, He would have appealed more readily to the human appetite for sensationalism. But He didn't do it that way. He wanted to walk among His people, to touch and heal their diseases, to hear their stories and speak to them of His Kingdom, to be with them. How He loved to be among people! That was always His desire. He always risked being rejected as ordinary in order to be accepted as a friend. When my turn came to go out and spread the good news, I thought to myself: If that's the way our Lord did it, then that's the way His followers should do it as well.

RESPOND

To be completely honest, Lord, I have to admit that I am often weighed down by problems — problems in the world, problems in my life, problems in my family. I know that You have chosen to save us by meeting us in the midst of our problems, but I also know that not all suffering is necessary, healthy, or desired by You. Help me to see the difference, so I can live in Your peace.

I never want to fall into an empty routine. I never want my faith to dim or my love to grow cold. Only You can keep my commitment fresh, Lord. And any of Your followers who are just going through the motions or who are giving in to selfishness: I pray for them now — especially your priests and consecrated souls. Keep their love fresh; stir their hearts with Your wisdom and zeal.

REST

You have given me such a treasure in my Catholic Faith. Show me how to share it. Often I don't know when to speak and when to stay silent. I don't know what others are thinking or suffering. But You do. You know exactly what everyone needs. Guide me; give me courage and simplicity. Make me a channel of Your peace.

RESOLVE

How can I carry this encounter with me into the day? (Write / Journal)

CLOSING PRAYER OF THANKSGIVING

Turn to page 9

DAY 21
TUESDAY

OCEAN OF MERCY

"O Christian, be aware of your nobility—it is God's own nature that you share; do not then, by an ignoble life, fall back into your former baseness." ~POPE ST. LEO THE GREAT

READ: MATTHEW 18:21-35

Then Peter went up to him and said, "Lord, how often must I forgive my brother if he wrongs me? As often as seven times?" Jesus answered, "Not seven, I tell you, but seventy-seven times. And so the kingdom of heaven may be compared to a king who decided to settle his accounts with his servants. When the reckoning began, they brought him a man who owed ten thousand talents; but he had no means of paying, so his master gave orders that he should be sold, together with his wife and children and all his possessions, to meet the debt. At this, the servant threw himself down at his master's feet. 'Give me time,' he said, 'and I will pay the whole sum.' And the servant's master felt so sorry for him that he let him go and canceled the debt. Now as this servant went out, he happened to meet a fellow servant who owed him one hundred denarii; and he seized him by the throat and began to throttle him. 'Pay what you owe me,' he said. His fellow servant fell at his feet and implored him, saying, 'Give me time and I will pay you.' But the other would not agree; on the contrary, he had him thrown into prison till he should pay the debt. His fellow servants were deeply distressed when they saw what had happened, and they went to their master and reported the whole affair to him. Then the master sent for him. 'You wicked servant,' he said, 'I canceled all that debt of yours when you appealed to me. Were you not bound, then, to have pity on your fellow servant just as I had pity on you?' And in his anger the master handed him over to the torturers till he should pay all his debt. And that is how my heavenly Father will deal with you unless you each forgive your brother from your heart."

REFLECT

This brilliant parable rightly convicts us of our repulsive self-righteousness, but we should not therefore overlook its illustration of Christ's magnanimity. Jesus Himself is the King who forgives the huge amount of ten thousand talents — an unimaginable, astronomical quantity of money. Likewise, Christ's compassion exceeds even the malice of His own murderers: "Father, forgive them, they know not what they do," He spoke from the Cross (Luke 23:34, NABRE).

Jesus: You can count on my forgiveness. You just need to do what this servant did: kneel down before me and ask for it. I know that sometimes it's hard for you to accept this forgiveness; your pride keeps you from forgiving yourself, so you hold my forgiveness at arm's length, or you doubt it. I don't want you to doubt my forgiveness. I want you to be absolutely sure. This is why I made it tangible in the sacrament of Reconciliation. When you come to me through the ministry of my chosen, ordained priest, you actually hear my own words speaking through his voice: "I absolve you from your sins." I invented this wonderful gift just for you, just so I could flood the depths of your misery with the ocean of my mercy.

RESPOND

It amazes me to think that I can always come to You; I can always ask You a question; You are always available. You never cease thinking of me. Like Peter, I can turn to You to resolve my doubts. Why do I turn to You so infrequently? Why do I forget about Your presence, Your guidance, Your passionate interest in my life?

Forgiveness is harder for me in some cases than in others. Some people who have wounded me really don't deserve to be forgiven, Lord. And yet You offer Your forgiveness to them. Why, then, do I resist? Free me from this snare of the devil. Teach me to forgive, no matter how I feel. Refresh my embittered heart. You love even those who have offended me terribly, and You can turn them into saints.

REST

Thank You for putting no limits on how much You would forgive me. Thank You for continuing to assure me of Your forgiveness through Confession.

There is no hesitancy in Your love for me, no holding back, no tinge of self-seeking. Why don't I trust You more? Jesus, teach me to trust You more.

RESOLVE

How can I carry this encounter with me into the day? (Write / Journal)

CLOSING PRAYER OF THANKSGIVING

Turn to page 9

DAY 22
WEDNESDAY

A MISSION IN LIFE
. . . .

"Of all divine things, the most godlike is to cooperate with
God in the conversion of sinners." ~ST. DENIS THE AREOPAGITE

READ: MATTHEW 5:17-19

"Do not imagine that I have come to abolish the Law or the Prophets. I have
come not to abolish but to complete them. I tell you solemnly, till heaven and
earth disappear, not one dot, not one little stroke, shall disappear from the
Law until its purpose is achieved. Therefore, the man who infringes even one
of the least of these commandments and teaches others to do the same will
be considered the least in the kingdom of heaven; but the man who keeps
them and teaches them will be considered great in the kingdom of heaven."

REFLECT

If any of Christ's other claims to ultimate authority leave room for doubt, the
one He makes here removes it completely. The Jews are aware that they are
God's Chosen People. Their individual and national identities stem from this
acute awareness. They trace the origin of their uniqueness to the covenant
God made with Moses: when God freed the ancient Hebrews from slavery
in Egypt, He established them as the Chosen People, and through Moses,
He gave them the Law as a kind of identification card. The Law of Moses,
then, was the mark of God's unique relationship with the Jewish people. In
His Sermon on the Mount, Jesus claims to bring that Law to its fulfillment.
In other words, He asserts Himself to be higher than the Law and therefore
able to explain the full meaning behind it — a meaning that the Jewish people
had previously failed to apprehend. If Christ puts Himself above the Law, and
the Law is God's own message to Israel, then clearly Jesus Christ is claiming
to have divine authority. Anyone who says otherwise has not understood
the Gospel or is trying to falsify it. Our Lord is also our God.

RESPOND

When I look into the bottom of my heart, Lord, I am not sure if I have really accepted my vocation to be a saint. Sometimes I think it's good enough just to be pretty good. It's not that I doubt your ability to make me into a saint, it's just that I doubt myself. Such idle fears! You created me for this, for this great mission, for this great love. And it's the only thing that matters. Lord Jesus, make me holy, and by my holiness may others open their hearts to You and the truth of who You are.

REST

When I consider my Christian responsibility to build up the Church, some aspects of that responsibility make me enthusiastic, as with any project that friends take on together, and some leave me cold, as with duties impersonally imposed from the outside. Why is this?

RESOLVE

How can I carry this encounter with me into the day? (Write / Journal)

CLOSING PRAYER OF THANKSGIVING

Turn to page 9

DAY 23
THURSDAY

A CLOSER LOOK AT THE DEVIL

"To choose rightly it is necessary to concentrate on the end for which I am created, that is, for the praise of God and for the salvation of my soul." ~ST. IGNATIUS OF LOYOLA

READ: LUKE 11:14-26

He was casting out a devil and it was dumb; but when the devil had gone out the dumb man spoke, and the people were amazed. But some of them said, "It is through Beelzebul, the prince of devils, that he casts out devils." Others asked him, as a test, for a sign from heaven; but, knowing what they were thinking, he said to them, "Every kingdom divided against itself is heading for ruin, and a household divided against itself collapses. So too with Satan: if he is divided against himself, how can his kingdom stand? — Since you assert that it is through Beelzebul that I cast out devils. Now if it is through Beelzebul that I cast out devils, through whom do your own experts cast them out? Let them be your judges then. But if it is through the finger of God that I cast out devils, then know that the kingdom of God has overtaken you. So long as a strong man fully armed guards his own palace, his goods are undisturbed; but when someone stronger than he is attacks and defeats him, the stronger man takes away all the weapons he relied on and shares out his spoil. He who is not with me is against me; and he who does not gather with me scatters. When an unclean spirit goes out of a man it wanders through waterless country looking for a place to rest, and not finding one it says, I will go back to the home I came from. But on arrival, finding it swept and tidied, it then goes off and brings seven other spirits more wicked than itself, and they go in and set up house there, so that the man ends up being worse than he was before."

REFLECT

Jesus is willing to discuss things with His enemies and with those who doubt, just as the Church is always ready to explain her teachings and listen to the problems and complaints of her children and inquirers. Jesus has been facing opposition since the beginning of His life, but He never loses patience, just as the Church is always willing to receive repentant sinners, no matter how many times they need to repent. Jesus teaches, forgives, invites, and sometimes warns, but He never closes the door to salvation. His love won't let Him. Even on the Cross, as His enemies taunt and deride Him, He still showers them with His patient and forgiving love: "Father, forgive them, they know not what they do" (Luke 23:34, NABRE). His whole life is one huge billboard: "You can trust in me no matter what."

RESPOND

Sometimes I hem and haw about what You are asking me. I ask for signs because I don't want to accept what I know Your will is. I don't know how You put up with me, Lord. Teach me humility and docility. Give me the strength and courage to follow You through thick and thin, trusting all the way.

I know that life is a battle between good and evil, but in the rush of everyday life, I forget about it. I don't want to live life on the surface! Save me from skimming along on fashionable and passing preoccupations. I want to go deeper. I want to discover and spread Your wisdom, Your goodness, and Your love.

REST

Patience is so hard for me. But You are perfect in Your patience, remaining in the tabernacle day after day. And You nourish me with Your own life, feeding my soul with Your virtues in Holy Communion. Activate in my heart the strength of Your virtue, so that all I do and say will draw others closer to You instead of pushing them away.

RESOLVE

How can I carry this encounter with me into the day? (Write / Journal)

CLOSING PRAYER OF THANKSGIVING

Turn to page 9

DAY 24
FRIDAY

LIFESTYLE BY CHRIST

"For our sakes he suffered all the agonies of body and mind, and did not shrink from any torment. He gave us a perfect example of patience and love." ~ST. FRANCIS OF PAOLA

READ: MARK 12:28-37

One of the scribes who had listened to them debating and had observed how well Jesus had answered them, now came up and put a question to him, "Which is the first of all the commandments?" Jesus replied, "This is the first: Listen, Israel, the Lord our God is the one Lord, and you must love the Lord your God with all your heart, with all your soul, with all your mind and with all your strength. The second is this: You must love your neighbor as yourself. There is no commandment greater than these." The scribe said to him, "Well spoken, Master; what you have said is true: that he is one and there is no other. To love him with all your heart, with all your understanding and strength, and to love your neighbor as yourself, this is far more important than any holocaust or sacrifice." Jesus, seeing how wisely he had spoken, said, "You are not far from the kingdom of God." And after that no one dared to question him any more.

Later, while teaching in the Temple, Jesus said, "How can the scribes maintain that the Christ is the son of David? David himself, moved by the Holy Spirit, said: 'The Lord said to my Lord: Sit at my right hand and I will put your enemies under your feet.' David himself calls him Lord, in what way then can he be his son?" And the great majority of the people heard this with delight.

REFLECT

This is the last in a series of questions that the "experts" in Jerusalem posed in order to discredit Jesus. Their efforts failed. In the end, "no one dared to question him anymore."

Sometimes we become so familiar with the figure of Christ as He appears in the Gospels that we forget the surpassing dignity and authority of His personality. If we were to meet Him on the street, we would immediately sense something about Him that set Him completely apart. If we were to engage in a conversation with Him in an airport waiting area or at a bus station, we would be impressed and attracted by the magnetism and quiet strength of His character. We should try to picture the marvelous figure of the Lord as He vanquishes Israel's most intelligent and powerful leaders in this battle of wits. These elite intellectuals and trendsetters intimidated the average citizen into obsequious obedience and cowering respect, but they met their match in the Lord.

RESPOND

You make things so simple, Lord. All I have to do is love God with all my strength and love my neighbor as myself. How I long to want only that in life! That is what You created me for. You are infinitely lovable, the source of all good things. And my neighbors — all my neighbors, without exception — are created by You and loved by You. O Jesus, make my heart overflow with love.

REST

Teach me to pray, Lord. I know I have asked You this before, but I ask again: really teach me to pray, please. I long for Your wisdom to shed its light in my mind. I long for Your love to inflame my heart. I long for Your strength to steel my weak will. You have called me to be Your apostle — now please, make me what You want me to be.

RESOLVE

How can I carry this encounter with me into the day? (Write / Journal)

CLOSING PRAYER OF THANKSGIVING

Turn to page 9

DAY 25
SATURDAY

THE ABCs OF SUCCESS

"Confession heals, confession justifies, confession grants pardon of sin. All hope consists in confession." ~ST. ISIDORE OF SEVILLE

READ: LUKE 18:9-17

He spoke the following parable to some people who prided themselves on being virtuous and despised everyone else, "Two men went up to the Temple to pray, one a Pharisee, the other a tax collector. The Pharisee stood there and said this prayer to himself, 'I thank you, God, that I am not grasping, unjust, adulterous like the rest of mankind, and particularly that I am not like this tax collector here. I fast twice a week; I pay tithes on all I get.' The tax collector stood some distance away, not daring even to raise his eyes to heaven; but he beat his breast and said, 'God, be merciful to me, a sinner.' This man, I tell you, went home again at rights with God; the other did not. For everyone who exalts himself will be humbled, but the man who humbles himself will be exalted." People even brought little children to him, for him to touch them; but when the disciples saw this they turned them away. But Jesus called the children to him and said, "Let the little children come to me, and do not stop them; for it is to such as these that the kingdom of God belongs. I tell you solemnly, anyone who does not welcome the kingdom of God like a little child will never enter it."

REFLECT

Jesus went after the big sinners — you don't get much bigger than "people who prided themselves on being virtuous and despised everyone else." He didn't just preach to the choir (which, in fact, is why His enemies had to have Him killed; His influence was simply becoming too widespread). This shows how much He cared about others and how little He worried about Himself. If He had been after comfortable self-satisfaction, He would never have gone after big sinners. This is confirmed by our own experience: When we don't go after those who need Christ most, isn't it because we care more about our own comfortable self-satisfaction than about expanding Christ's Kingdom? Christ's concern for big sinners also gives us another reason to trust Him without limits. No sinner is too big for Christ's mercy. His mercy is infinite, vast like an ocean; even the greatest sins are finite, like a thimble. How foolish we would be to think our thimble was too deep for His ocean!

RESPOND

You are my Lord. I understand what that means: I owe everything to You. You hold my entire existence in the palm of Your hand. You never cease thinking of me and drawing me closer to You. You are my Lord, but You are also my Father, my Brother, and my Friend. Jesus, I trust in You.

I ask You to have mercy on me, for all my selfishness I know about and for all my selfishness I'm unaware of. And I ask You to have mercy on all sinners. It is Your mercy that makes Your glory shine! Teach me to confide in Your mercy no matter what, and to be merciful, forgiving, gentle, and meek — especially with those who don't deserve it.

REST

Pour Your courage into my heart, Lord. I am hampered in my apostolate and my testimony because I still care too much about what other people will think. I'm glad you didn't give in to those temptations. Teach me to be adventurous in building Your Kingdom and spreading it, even to the "big sinners" who seem so hopeless.

RESOLVE

How can I carry this encounter with me into the day? (Write / Journal)

CLOSING PRAYER OF THANKSGIVING

Turn to page 9

DAY 26
FOURTH SUNDAY OF LENT

A BLIND MAN SEES

"Let us carry bravely the shield of faith, so that
with its protection we may be able to parry
whatever the enemy hurls at us." — St. Cyprian

READ: JOHN 9:1–17

As he went along, he saw a man who had been blind from birth. His disciples asked him, "Rabbi, who sinned, this man or his parents, for him to have been born blind?" "Neither he nor his parents sinned," Jesus answered, "he was born blind so that the works of God might be displayed in him. As long as the day lasts I must carry out the work of the one who sent me; the night will soon be here when no one can work. As long as I am in the world I am the light of the world." Having said this, he spat on the ground, made a paste with the spittle, put this over the eyes of the blind man, and said to him, "Go and wash in the Pool of Siloam (a name that means 'sent')." So the blind man went off and washed himself, and came away with his sight restored.

His neighbors and people who earlier had seen him begging said, "Isn't this the man who used to sit and beg?" Some said, "Yes, it is the same one." Others said, "No, he only looks like him." The man himself said, "I am the man." So they said to him, "Then how do your eyes come to be open?" "The man called Jesus," he answered, "made a paste, dabbed my eyes with it and said to me, 'Go and wash at Siloam'; so I went, and when I washed I could see." They asked, "Where is he?" "I don't know," he answered. They brought the man who had been blind to the Pharisees. It had been a sabbath day when Jesus made the paste and opened the man's eyes, so when the Pharisees asked him how he had come to see, he said, "He put a paste on my eyes, and I washed, and I can see." Then some of the Pharisees said, "This man cannot be from God: he does not keep the sabbath." Others said, "How could a sinner produce signs like this?" And there was disagreement among them. So they spoke to the blind man again, "What have you to say about him yourself, now that he has opened your eyes?" "He is a prophet," replied the man.

REFLECT

Among the many lessons hidden in this passage, one deserves special mention. How odd that Jesus used spittle and mud to make clay, put the clay on the man's eyelids, and told him to go to the pool of Siloam to wash! Did He have to perform the miracle like that? Certainly not: He could have merely snapped His fingers (He is God, after all). Yet it was appropriate to do so. Why? Besides the obvious reason that in ancient times saliva was often used in medical procedures, through this method of curing, the blind man felt Christ touching Him, heard His voice, and actively participated in the saving deed of God. In this way, Christ shows how He communicates God's grace to us in ways appropriate to our human nature — which includes both body and spirit. Jesus wants to reach into our lives, to lower Himself to our level, to touch us, even physically. Christ's touch gave the blind man hope and confidence, making the miracle into a personal encounter, not a magic trick. The Catholic Church, under the constant guidance of the Holy Spirit, has preserved this method of administering God's grace through the sacraments. The priest's words of absolution at the end of Confession provide the consolation we need to bring the reality of God's forgiveness home to our hearts. The water of Baptism, the bread and wine of the Eucharist, the chrism — all the material elements of the sacraments — extend throughout time the reality of God's eager desire to reach out and touch us. We are not purely spiritual beings; it suits us to encounter God through the mediation of physical realities. God became man not to despoil our humanity but to bring it to its fullness.

RESPOND

Too frequently, I take Your sacraments for granted. You are so humble and gentle; You want to pour the balm of Your grace into my life through signs that I can recognize and understand. I want to be grateful and attentive to Your gifts. I want to appreciate them as I should and teach others to do the same. Open my eyes, Lord.

REST

Never let me forget your majesty and your glory. This world seems to delight in watering down Your magnificence. But I believe in Your greatness and

Your goodness. I want to live in the reality of Your presence, like the saints. I want to learn to hear Your voice calling out to me in all things, as I know You are doing, because You have promised that Your love for me is constant, personal, and determined.

RESOLVE

How can I carry this encounter with me into the day? (Write / Journal)

CLOSING PRAYER OF THANKSGIVING

Turn to page 9

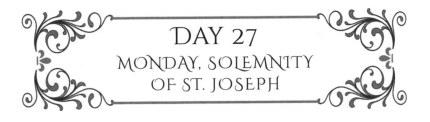

DAY 27
MONDAY, SOLEMNITY
OF ST. JOSEPH

SALVATION IS BORN

"What is this wealth of goodness? What is this mystery that touches me? I received the divine image and I did not keep it. He receives my flesh to save the image and grant immortality to the flesh. This, his second communion with us, is far more marvelous than the first." ~ST. GREGORY NAZIANZEN, ORATION 45

READ: MATTHEW 1:18-25

This is how Jesus Christ came to be born. His mother Mary was betrothed to Joseph; but before they came to live together she was found to be with child through the Holy Spirit. Her husband Joseph, being a man of honor and wanting to spare her publicity, decided to divorce her informally. He had made up his mind to do this when the angel of the Lord appeared to him in a dream and said, "Joseph son of David, do not be afraid to take Mary home as your wife, because she has conceived what is in her by the Holy Spirit. She will give birth to a son and you must name him Jesus, because he is the one who is to save his people from their sins."

Now all this took place to fulfill the words spoken by the Lord through the prophet: "The virgin will conceive and give birth to a son and they will call him Emmanuel, a name which means 'God-is-with-us.'" When Joseph woke up he did what the angel of the Lord had told him to do: he took his wife to his home and, though he had not had intercourse with her, she gave birth to a son; and he named him Jesus.

REFLECT

God is all powerful, and He could have saved us in any number of ways. He chose the Incarnation: becoming one of us. Such an uncomfortable choice — at least, it certainly upset Joseph's plans. But God is not obliged to act within the parameters of our personal comfort zones. He has said as much Himself: "As the heavens are higher than the earth, so are my ways higher than your ways, my thoughts higher than your thoughts" (Isa. 55:9, NABRE). Joseph finds his betrothed pregnant. He knows her virtue and can't imagine what happened. It seems she is not free to tell him, or if she does tell him, he finds it hard to accept, so Mary has to trust that God will work it out. After a period of anxiety and confusion, an angel appears, only to give Joseph some short-term instructions. Why didn't God simply explain it all beforehand — send a letter with the whole plan mapped out step by step? Why did the ancient prophecies leave so much room for interpretation? God is the Lord; He acts according to His own wisdom and love, and we follow Him "by faith, not by sight" (2 Cor. 5:7, NABRE). If at times following the Lord was uncomfortable even for Joseph and Mary, we can expect nothing less for ourselves.

RESPOND

Many times I resent when my plans are foiled and my hopes left unfulfilled. When You throw me curve balls, I get nervous, or angry, or doubtful. And yet I know that You are always guiding me with Your infinite wisdom. Teach me to discover Your will in the midst of life's ups and downs and to be docile, like Joseph and Mary. Thy Kingdom come, Lord — not mine.

REST

So often I depend almost entirely on my own talents and strength to succeed. And yet here You are, teaching me by Your quiet coming to earth, that when it comes to the only success that really matters, success as a human being, as a child of God, I am helpless! I need You, Lord, to be my Savior. I need Your love and Your grace to give meaning and direction to my life. Grant me success, Lord, the kind that lasts forever.

RESOLVE

How can I carry this encounter with me into the day? (Write / Journal)

CLOSING PRAYER OF THANKSGIVING

Turn to page 9

DAY 28
TUESDAY

STIRRING THINGS UP
....

"Whether I receive good or ill, I return thanks
equally to God, who taught me always to
trust him unreservedly." ~ST. PATRICK

READ: JOHN 5:1-18

Some time after this there was a Jewish festival, and Jesus went up to Jerusalem.

Now at the Sheep Pool in Jerusalem there is a building, called Bethzatha in Hebrew, consisting of five porticos; and under these were crowds of sick people — blind, lame, paralyzed — waiting for the water to move; for at intervals the angel of the Lord came down into the pool, and the water was disturbed, and the first person to enter the water after this disturbance was cured of any ailment he suffered from. One man there had an illness which had lasted thirty-eight years, and when Jesus saw him lying there and knew he had been in this condition for a long time, he said, "Do you want to be well again?" "Sir," replied the sick man, "I have no one to put me into the pool when the water is disturbed; and while I am still on the way, someone else gets there before me." Jesus said, "Get up, pick up your sleeping-mat and walk." The man was cured at once, and he picked up his mat and walked away.

Now that day happened to be the sabbath, so the Jews said to the man who had been cured, "It is the sabbath; you are not allowed to carry your sleeping-mat." He replied, "But the man who cured me told me, 'Pick up your mat and walk.'" They asked "Who is the man who said to you, 'Pick up your mat and walk'?" The man had no idea who it was, since Jesus had disappeared into the crowd that filled the place. After a while Jesus met him in the Temple and said, "Now you are well again, be sure not to sin any more, or something worse may happen to you." The man went back and told the Jews that it was Jesus who had cured him. It was because he did things like this on the sabbath that the Jews began to persecute Jesus. His answer to them was, "My Father goes on working, and so do I." But that only made the Jews even more intent on killing him, because, not content with breaking the sabbath, he spoke of God as his own Father, and so made himself God's equal.

REFLECT

This man had been ill for thirty-eight years. It seems from Jesus' later comment when they meet in the Temple that his own sins had been the cause of his illness. It was an illness that made him an invalid, helpless and incapable of contributing to the society around him. And to top it all off, he was a lonely man. He didn't have any friend or family member who could help him down to the pool after the stirring of the waters. And then one day, a young rabbi comes up to him. He squats down beside him, looks into his eyes, and asks him if he wants to be cured. Jesus is always taking the initiative in our lives. He knows what we need more than we do. He knows how much we have suffered and how our sins have damaged our souls. He comes to heal and renew us.

The sick man: Of course I wanted to be cured. That's why I was still waiting at the pool. It seemed an odd question to me. So I looked up at this man. I looked into His eyes as I told Him that I wasn't fast enough to make it to the healing waters. What I said didn't seem to matter. He looked at me intently but gently. I don't know how else to describe it. And then He seemed to smile, and there was a fire in His eyes. And He told me to get up, pick up my sleeping mat, and walk. I thought to myself, "Doesn't He see that I can't get up, that I can't carry anything, let alone my sleeping mat? I can't even walk! Doesn't He see me?" For thirty-eight years I had been lame, unable to do any of those things, and this man was telling me to stand up. It was a crazy thing to say. But His eyes weren't crazy. He just kept looking at me intently. I was going to tell Him what a crazy idea it was, but His eyes wouldn't let me. Somehow, the fire in His eyes kindled one in my own, and all of a sudden, I knew that I just had to do what He was telling me. But how could I? I had to try. Even as part of me objected — it was such an absurd thing that He was saying — I couldn't help but start to hope. And He kept looking at me and, well, I don't know how it happened, but I just started to get up, and all of a sudden, I could. And then I picked up my mat. And I started walking. After thirty-eight years! I turned to thank Him — but He was gone.

RESPOND

Why didn't the leaders of Jerusalem believe in You? They saw Your miracles, but even that couldn't pry their hearts away from their self-centeredness. It seems so unreasonable. And yet can I say that my faith is robust and confident? Am I not like those leaders, unable to free myself from my self-centeredness, in spite of all You have done for me? Teach me, Lord, to do Your will. Increase my faith.

Many times, the little things You ask me to do seem impossible. How can I be patient and kind to people who irritate me, who are ungrateful? How can I overcome the repugnance I feel sometimes in the face of my responsibilities? How can I simply trust You when so many things go wrong and nothing seems to work? Lord, I believe in You. If you tell me to get up and walk, I will. Thy will be done.

REST

I want to be as generous as You are, Lord. You saw this man, knew his suffering, and came to his rescue. You have made me Your ambassador; You want me to do the same for everyone around me. You want me to keep my eyes open for opportunities to serve, help, and do good. You want me to make that my obsession, as it was Yours. Give me Your grace, Lord, so that I, too, can "go on working."

RESOLVE

How can I carry this encounter with me into the day? (Write / Journal)

CLOSING PRAYER OF THANKSGIVING

Turn to page 9

DAY 29
WEDNESDAY

AIMING AT GOD'S WILL

"There is one most priceless pearl: the knowledge
of the Savior, the mystery of his Passion, the
secret of his Resurrection." ~ST. JEROME

READ: JOHN 5:19-30

To this accusation Jesus replied· "I tell you most solemnly, the Son can
do nothing by himself; he can do only what he sees the Father doing: and
whatever the Father does the Son does too. For the Father loves the Son and
shows him everything he does himself, and he will show him even greater
things than these, works that will astonish you. Thus, as the Father raises
the dead and gives them life, so the Son gives life to anyone he chooses; for
the Father judges no one; he has entrusted all judgment to the Son, so that
all may honor the Son as they honor the Father. Whoever refuses honor to
the Son refuses honor to the Father who sent him. I tell you most solemnly,
whoever listens to my words, and believes in the one who sent me, has eternal
life; without being brought to judgment he has passed from death to life. I tell
you most solemnly, the hour will come — in fact it is here already — when
the dead will hear the voice of the Son of God, and all who hear it will live.
For the Father, who is the source of life, has made the Son the source of life;
and, because he is the Son of Man, has appointed him supreme judge. Do
not be surprised at this, for the hour is coming when the dead will leave their
graves at the sound of his voice: those who did good will rise again to life;
and those who did evil, to condemnation. I can do nothing by myself; I can
only judge as I am told to judge, and my judging is just, because my aim is
to do not my own will, but the will of him who sent me."

REFLECT

Jesus wants only one thing — for us to have life. Death was the consequence
of Original Sin and continues to be the consequence of all sins. Spiritual

death ensues from sin because sin is rebellion against God, a willful separation of oneself from communion, from friendship, with God. But since God alone is the source of all life, separation from Him means separation from life, from the fullness of that meaningful and fruitful life that He created us to experience. And if friendship with God is not reestablished while one's earthly, biological life lasts, the separation from God will endure in an eternal "condemnation." But those who believe and trust in Jesus regain communion and friendship with God, so they can be reborn to a meaningful and fruitful life here on earth. And if they stay faithful to their friendship with God until the end of their earthly sojourn, they will "rise again to life" at the end of history, and they will enjoy that friendship for all eternity.

Jesus: When I look at you and think of you, which I am always doing, I picture you living the life I created you to live. I know that now you still struggle and suffer, but this is only a passing stage. You are still recovering from sin. You are still in rehabilitation, and that always hurts. Keep going. Keep seeking my will. Keep getting up every time you fall. I am right at your side. I am leading you to a life that will fill you with more joy and wisdom and love than you can possibly imagine. I am the life, and I want you to spend forever with me.

RESPOND

When I try to understand You, Lord, I am blinded by the immensity of Your mystery. And yet I know that You came to earth and walked among men and that You continue to stay with me now in Your Church and through Your sacraments precisely because You didn't want to keep Your distance. You want me to know You. Little by little, Lord, reveal Yourself to me. Open my eyes; I want to see Your glory.

REST

I know that You want to give me eternal life. You want to give me what I yearn for, passionately, in the very core of my being. You created me for that. But You can give it to me only if I am willing to follow You, if I am willing to seek and fulfill Your will, no matter what. I want to, Lord. I want to spend my days doing good for those around me, just as You did, helping others to find life in You, now and for all eternity.

RESOLVE
How can I carry this encounter with me into the day? (Write / Journal)

CLOSING PRAYER OF THANKSGIVING

Turn to page 9

DAY 30
THURSDAY

EASY TO PLEASE

"This love for Christ must ever be the chiefest
and most agreeable result of a knowledge
of Holy Scripture." ~POPE BENEDICT XV

READ: JOHN 5:31-47

"Were I to testify on my own behalf, my testimony would not be valid; but there is another witness who can speak on my behalf, and I know that his testimony is valid. You sent messengers to John, and he gave his testimony to the truth: not that I depend on human testimony; no, it is for your salvation that I speak of this. John was a lamp alight and shining and for a time you were content to enjoy the light that he gave. But my testimony is greater than John's: the works my Father has given me to carry out, these same works of mine testify that the Father has sent me. Besides, the Father who sent me bears witness to me himself. You have never heard his voice, you have never seen his shape, and his word finds no home in you because you do not believe in the one he has sent. You study the scriptures, believing that in them you have eternal life; now these same scriptures testify to me, and yet you refuse to come to me for life! As for human approval, this means nothing to me. Besides, I know you too well: you have no love of God in you. I have come in the name of my Father and you refuse to accept me; if someone else comes in his own name you will accept him. How can you believe, since you look to one another for approval and are not concerned with the approval that comes from the one God? Do not imagine that I am going to accuse you before the Father: you place your hopes on Moses, and Moses will be your accuser. If you really believed him you would believe me too, since it was I that he was writing about; but if you refuse to believe what he wrote, how can you believe what I say?"

REFLECT

Jesus is a faithful friend. Once again, He publicly praises John the Baptist, who had dedicated his life to serving Christ and bearing Him witness. Jesus never forgets deeds done to please Him and build up His Kingdom. He is interested in everything we do because He loves us more than the most loving parent, more than the most faithful spouse. He appreciates every effort we make in His name, for His sake. How much confidence this should give us! Even if no one ever knows or sees our sacrifices, our small acts of self-denial and self-giving, Jesus is gathering them up like beautiful flowers and enjoying each one of them. Each one weaves the patchwork of our life. How much freedom this truth can give to our souls! We no longer have to scratch and fight our way to the honors platform in order to win prizes that perish and recognition that withers. In Christ, we can flourish without fear.

Jesus: My love is enough for you. Live in the light of my love. Live for loving me. Seek my approval in all you do; I am so easy to please, and no whims or selfishness or bad moods cloud my appreciation. I lived and died and rose for you. I want to give you the kind of peace and joy that doesn't wear away. All you need is my love.

RESPOND

I believe in You, Lord, but I know so many people who don't believe in You. They are still looking for meaning in awards and money and reputation. They are stuck on that thankless merry-go-round. Thank You for taking me off that and putting me on the path of life. Forgive me for my ingratitude, for the times I resent Your demands. Make me Your disciple, Your spokesperson, to bring many others to Your friendship.

REST

Sometimes I am afraid that I am not doing enough for You, Lord. That's because I keep thinking that I need to earn Your love the way I have had to earn the love of others. But You are not like that. You already love me, and nothing I do can increase or decrease that love. Cast out my fears and fill me with the courage and energy that come from knowing I am loved unconditionally and infinitely by You.

RESOLVE

How can I carry this encounter with me into the day? (Write / Journal)

CLOSING PRAYER OF THANKSGIVING

Turn to page 9

DAY 31
FRIDAY

CONFLICT AND CONTRADICTION

"When we consider that Christ is the true light far removed from all falsehood, we realize that our lives too should be lit by the rays of the sun of justice, which shine for our enlightenment. These rays are the virtues." ~ST. GREGORY OF NYSSA

READ: JOHN 7:20-36

"Why do you want to kill me?" The crowd replied, "You are mad! Who wants to kill you?" Jesus answered, "One work I did, and you are all surprised by it. Moses ordered you to practise circumcision — not that it began with him, it goes back to the patriarchs — and you circumcise on the sabbath. Now if a man can be circumcised on the sabbath so that the Law of Moses is not broken, why are you angry with me for making a man whole and complete on a sabbath? Do not keep judging according to appearances; let your judgement be according to what is right." Meanwhile some of the people of Jerusalem were saying, "Isn't this the man they want to kill? And here he is, speaking freely, and they have nothing to say to him! Can it be true the authorities have made up their minds that he is the Christ? Yet we all know where he comes from, but when the Christ appears no one will know where he comes from." Then, as Jesus taught in the Temple, he cried out: "Yes, you know me and you know where I came from. Yet I have not come of myself: no, there is one who sent me and I really come from him, and you do not know him, but I know him because I have come from him and it was he who sent me." They would have arrested him then, but because his time had not yet come no one laid a hand on him. There were many people in the crowds, however, who believed in him; they were saying, "When the Christ comes, will he give more signs than this man?" Hearing that rumors like this about him were spreading among the people, the Pharisees sent the Temple police to arrest him. Then Jesus said: "I shall remain with you for only a short time now; then I shall go back to the one who sent me. You will look for me and will not find me: where I am you cannot come." The Jews then said to one another, "Where is he going that we shan't be able to find him? Is he going abroad to the people who are dispersed among the Greeks and will he teach the Greeks? What does he mean when he says: 'You will look for me and will not find me: where I am, you cannot come?'"

REFLECT

A touch of sadness seems to color Jesus' words when the guards show up to arrest Him. The time for His Passion has not yet arrived, however, and so they do not arrest Him. But their arrival makes Jesus think ahead to what He knows will happen in just a few months. He is painfully aware that His time is limited. We can hear the longing in His voice as He alludes to His Ascension — He wants people to believe in Him before their hearts become too hardened to believe. Jesus still longs for us to believe in Him, to trust Him, to accept Him. Life is so short; time is so limited. God showers every soul with His graces and invitations, but still many souls refuse to believe.

Christ: You are a comfort to me. You have listened to my voice in your conscience, and you have followed me. You have trusted me. You have let me heal you and guide you with my grace. I am preparing a place for you in my Father's house. But I wish I could describe to you how it pains my heart to see so many souls turn their backs on me. What more could I have done for them? Each one of them is looking for me, but they keep looking in the wrong places. And the farther they distance themselves from me, the less distinct my voice becomes. Go to them and tell them that I am what they are looking for. I will be with you.

RESPOND

Keep my heart open to You, Lord. It's so easy to go to the right or to the left, to fall into legalism or laxity, like the Pharisees and the Sadducees, those leaders of Jerusalem who tried to destroy You. Keep me on the right path, Lord. Teach me to do Your will. Teach me to keep striving to love You with all my heart and to love my neighbor as myself. Push me, Lord; draw me closer to You.

I praise You for Your gentle love. You come to me in the simple things of life. It delights You to show Your love and Your majesty in the quiet beauty of a sunset, the simple joy of a child's smile, the embrace of a loved one, the refreshing caress of a cool breeze. Teach me the wisdom I need to live in constant contact with You, so I can be a channel of Your grace.

REST

I know I have only a little time left on this earth. I want to do so much. But my job is not to save the world — that's Your job, Lord. All I have to do is fulfill Your will with trust and love. I ask only that You make Your will clear to me each day and then give me the strength to carry it out with love. When my last day comes, I want to be able to say: I love You Lord, and that's why I always sought to do Your will.

RESOLVE

How can I carry this encounter with me into the day? (Write / Journal)

CLOSING PRAYER OF THANKSGIVING

Turn to page 9

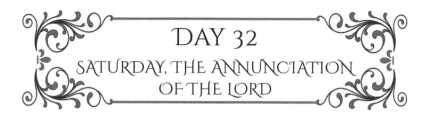

DAY 32
SATURDAY, THE ANNUNCIATION OF THE LORD

THE GREATEST YES

"Therefore, though it is God who takes the initiative of coming to dwell in the midst of men, and he is always the main architect of this plan, it is also true that he does not will to carry it out without our active cooperation." ~POPE BENEDICT XVI

READ: LUKE 1:26-38

In the sixth month the angel Gabriel was sent by God to a town in Galilee called Nazareth, to a virgin betrothed to a man named Joseph, of the House of David; and the virgin's name was Mary. He went in and said to her, "Rejoice, so highly favoured! The Lord is with you." She was deeply disturbed by these words and asked herself what this greeting could mean, but the angel said to her, "Mary, do not be afraid; you have won God's favour. Listen! You are to conceive and bear a son, and you must name him Jesus. He will be great and will be called Son of the Most High. The Lord God will give him the throne of his ancestor David; he will rule over the House of Jacob for ever and his reign will have no end." Mary said to the angel, "But how can this come about, since I am a virgin?" "The Holy Spirit will come upon you," the angel answered, "and the power of the Most High will cover you with its shadow. And so the child will be holy and will be called Son of God. Know this too: your kinswoman Elizabeth has, in her old age, herself conceived a son, and she whom people called barren is now in her sixth month, for nothing is impossible to God." "I am the handmaid of the Lord," said Mary; "let what you have said be done to me." And the angel left her.

REFLECT

Many friends exchange gifts, but only Christ has given us His own Mother to be our solace and our refuge as we strive to follow in His footsteps.

As He was dying on the Cross, Jesus entrusted His Mother to the care of His "beloved disciple," and He entrusted the disciple to her care: "When Jesus saw his mother and the disciple there whom he loved, he said to his mother, 'Woman, behold, your son.' Then he said to the disciple, 'Behold, your mother.' And from that hour the disciple took her into his home" (John 19:26–27, NABRE).

From its earliest days, the Church has interpreted this passage in a deeply spiritual way: since Jesus has desired to have us as His brothers and sisters, He has also desired to share with us His Mother, to give us a mother in the order of grace. Through the ages, Christians in all walks of life have been inspired by Mary's example, comforted by her spiritual solicitude, and aided by her heavenly intercession. Wherever one finds true devotion to Mary (which consists primarily in the imitation of her yes to God, not just in pious expressions and pretty pictures), one finds as well a passionate love for Jesus Christ, the Savior. She accompanied Jesus on every step of His earthly sojourn, and she accompanies His little brothers and sisters (that's us) with equal love and concern.

RESPOND

Mary, you were just a girl when God came and invited you to be the Mother of the Savior. Even then, you knew that God's will was the highest and wisest calling. You didn't fear missing out on all that the world had to offer because you wanted only to stay close to the world's Creator. Teach me to trust and love Christ, and teach me to give Him to others, as you gave Him to us.

REST

How strange, Lord, that You made the history of salvation depend not only on Your own actions but also on the free cooperation of Your creatures! You waited for Mary to say yes before coming to be our Savior. You wait for each of us to say yes before coming to save us. I renew my yes right now. Teach me to help others say yes too; only what I do for Your Kingdom will last forever.

RESOLVE

How can I carry this encounter with me into the day? (Write / Journal)

CLOSING PRAYER OF THANKSGIVING

Turn to page 9

DAY 33
FIFTH SUNDAY OF LENT

THE FORCE OF FAITH — THE POWER OF LOVE

"Since Christ is our peace, we shall be living up to the name of Christian if we let Christ be seen in our lives by letting peace reign in our hearts." ~ST. GREGORY OF NYSSA

READ: JOHN 11:17-44

On arriving, Jesus found that Lazarus had been in the tomb for four days already. Bethany is only about two miles from Jerusalem, and many Jews had come to Martha and Mary to sympathize with them over their brother. When Martha heard that Jesus had come she went to meet him. Mary remained sitting in the house. Martha said to Jesus, "If you had been here, my brother would not have died, but I know that, even now, whatever you ask of God, he will grant you." "Your brother," said Jesus to her, "will rise again." Martha said, "I know he will rise again at the resurrection on the last day." Jesus said: "I am the resurrection. If anyone believes in me, even though he dies he will live, and whoever lives and believes in me will never die. Do you believe this?" "Yes, Lord," she said, "I believe that you are the Christ, the Son of God, the one who was to come into this world." When she had said this, she went and called her sister Mary, saying in a low voice, "The Master is here and wants to see you." Hearing this, Mary got up quickly and went to him. Jesus had not yet come into the village; he was still at the place where Martha had met him. When the Jews who were in the house sympathizing with Mary saw her get up so quickly and go out, they followed her, thinking that she was going to the tomb to weep there. Mary went to Jesus, and as soon as she saw him she threw herself at his feet, saying, "Lord, if you had been here, my brother would not have died." At the sight of her tears, and those of the Jews who followed her, Jesus said in great distress, with a sigh that came straight from the heart, "Where have you put him?" They said, "Lord, come and see." Jesus wept; and the Jews said, "See how much he loved him!" But there were some who remarked, "He opened the eyes of the blind man, could he not have prevented this man's death?" Still sighing, Jesus reached the tomb: it was a cave with a stone to close the opening. Jesus said, "Take the stone away." Martha said to him, "Lord, by now he will smell; this is the fourth day." Jesus replied, "Have I not told you that if you believe you will see the glory of God?" So they took away the stone. Then Jesus lifted up his eyes and said: "Father, I thank you for hearing my prayer. I knew indeed that you always hear me, but I speak for the sake of all these who stand round me, so that they may believe it was you who sent me." When he had said this, he cried in a loud voice, "Lazarus, here! Come out!" The dead man came out, his feet and hands bound with bands of stuff and a cloth round his face. Jesus said to them, "Unbind him, let him go free."

REFLECT

This passage contains the shortest verse in the New Testament: "Jesus wept." Jesus Christ is not a distant God. Look how intimately and familiarly Martha and Mary treat Him! He never relinquishes His Lordship, and they never forget that He is the Lord. But He is unlike any other lord: He not only gives us protection, security, life, and peace; He gives us His very heart. The heart of Christ yearns for us to give Him as much love and confidence as Mary and Martha did; He yearns to be let into the presence of our hearts so as to share our sorrows and troubles. "Jesus wept." No other god ever shared our tears; only Christ is Emmanuel, "God with us."

RESPOND

Teach me to be as close to You as Mary and Martha were. Teach me to speak to You right from my heart, to share all my thoughts with You. Teach me to be sincere and spontaneous yet still full of reverence and respect. I, too, believe in You; I know that You are the Resurrection; You are the life. Teach me to trust in You and to do Your will.

REST

Do You still weep with me, Lord? Do You still feel the losses I feel, the struggles that weigh me down? Can You understand them? Can You come and rescue me from my sorrow, as You did with Mary and Martha? I know You do, and I know You can. O Lord, increase my faith! Increase my faith! Increase my faith! You don't want me to suffer alone. Let me know Your presence, Lord.

RESOLVE
How can I carry this encounter with me into the day? (Write / Journal)

CLOSING PRAYER OF THANKSGIVING

Turn to page 9

GETTING WHAT WE DON'T DESERVE

"His attitude towards sinners was full of kindness and loving friendship." ~ST. JOHN BOSCO

READ: JOHN 8:2-11

At daybreak he appeared in the Temple again; and as all the people came to him, he sat down and began to teach them. The scribes and Pharisees brought a woman along who had been caught committing adultery; and making her stand there in full view of everybody, they said to Jesus, "Master, this woman was caught in the very act of committing adultery, and Moses has ordered us in the Law to condemn women like this to death by stoning. What have you to say?" They asked him this as a test, looking for something to use against him. But Jesus bent down and started writing on the ground with his finger. As they persisted with their question, he looked up and said, "If there is one of you who has not sinned, let him be the first to throw a stone at her." Then he bent down and wrote on the ground again. When they heard this they went away one by one, beginning with the eldest, until Jesus was left alone with the woman, who remained standing there. He looked up and said, "Woman, where are they? Has no one condemned you?" "No one, sir," she replied. "Neither do I condemn you," said Jesus, "go away, and don't sin any more."

REFLECT

Jesus: I came not to condemn the world, but to save the world. If I just wanted to condemn you, I would have had no reason to come. I know your sins and your weakness, and still I called you and continue to call you. Think for a moment about the one reason behind my Incarnation, my life, my Passion, my death, my Resurrection, and my Ascension. Why would I follow such an itinerary? It was only because I want your friendship.

Every page and word of the Gospels, every faithful action and teaching of my Church has one, single purpose: to convince you that I want to walk with you now and spend eternity showing you the splendors of my Kingdom. I am all for you, and I ask in return only one thing, the same thing I asked of this adulterous woman: trust me, accept my love, and turn away from your sin.

RESPOND

Make me a channel of Your mercy, Lord. Your mercy means that even when I offend You, You keep on loving me and wanting what's best for me. I want to be like that. I want to be like gravity: continually pulling, no matter what; I want to keep on showing people Your goodness and wisdom. I want to keep on leading them to You, to keep on loving even those I find hard to love. Forgive me, Lord, for judging my neighbor. How foolish it is for me to pass judgment and criticize and pigeonhole! Can I see others' hearts? The Pharisees were quick to condemn because it made them feel important and superior. But I am even quicker to make excuses for myself and my failings. Teach me to see others as You see them and to speak about them as I would want them to speak about me.

REST

I want to be able to defend Your truth and the teachings of Your Church, but so often I am at a loss for words. In the midst of conversations and encounters, I get flustered. Afterward, I think up great responses. You always had the right response. You always knew what to say. Fill me with Your grace and Your wisdom, Lord, so that I can be Your faithful friend and true ambassador.

RESOLVE

How can I carry this encounter with me into the day? (Write / Journal)

CLOSING PRAYER OF THANKSGIVING

Turn to page 9

DAY 35
TUESDAY

CHRIST'S PROGRAM OF LIFE

"For God, as I have said, does not work in those
who refuse to place all their trust and expectation
in him alone." ~ST. JEROME EMILIANI

READ: JOHN 8:21-30

Again he said to them: "I am going away; you will look for me and you will die in your sin. Where I am going, you cannot come." The Jews said to one another, "Will he kill himself? Is that what he means by saying, 'Where I am going, you cannot come?'" Jesus went on: "You are from below; I am from above. You are of this world; I am not of this world. I have told you already: You will die in your sins. Yes, if you do not believe that I am He, you will die in your sins." So they said to him, "Who are you?" Jesus answered: "What I have told you from the outset. About you I have much to say and much to condemn; but the one who sent me is truthful, and what I have learnt from him I declare to the world." They failed to understand that he was talking to them about the Father. So Jesus said: "When you have lifted up the Son of Man, then you will know that I am He and that I do nothing of myself: what the Father has taught me is what I preach; he who sent me is with me, and has not left me to myself, for I always do what pleases him." As he was saying this, many came to believe in him.

REFLECT

Jesus: I and my Father are one. When I called you to be my disciple, I called you to live in communion with me, just as I do with my Father. And just as my Father "is with me, and has not left me to myself," I am always with you, and I will never abandon you. In your heart, you know this, but even so, you often let yourself be carried away by worries and fears. When I let a cloud block out the sun, does the sun disappear? The sun is always there, and just so, I am always watching over you. Every worry and fear that comes across the sky of your soul is a chance for you to exercise your faith and trust in me. That is what pleases me, and that is what sets my grace free to transform you and strengthen you and release your full potential for living as you ought to live. Seek always to do what pleases me, as I always sought to do what was pleasing to my Father, and you will discover anew my presence and grace, over and over again.

RESPOND

I, too, am sometimes hard-hearted, like the Pharisees and the scribes, who loved their own plans so much that they couldn't even see Your plan. Cure me, Lord. Purify my heart. Show me my prejudices and selfish tendencies. Shine the light of Your love into all the shadows of my soul. I want to be completely Yours. I want to become Your faithful disciple, a soldier You can count on.

How simple Your program of life is! You seek always and everywhere to do what is pleasing to the Father. Teach me to live like that. Free me from my obsession with pleasing myself. You didn't design me to find fulfillment in navel-gazing; You created me to flourish through self-forgetting love. With the love of Your heart, Lord, inflame my heart.

REST

Are You really always with me? Why do You let me feel alone? Why do You let so many clouds block out the sun? You want me to grow up, to mature. You want me to love You for You and not for the light and gifts that You give to me. You want me to exercise the precious virtues of faith, hope, and love, which have to be based on trust. Teach me to leave behind my cold calculations and abandon myself to Your goodness.

RESOLVE

How can I carry this encounter with me into the day? (Write / Journal)

CLOSING PRAYER OF THANKSGIVING

Turn to page 9

HOME FREE

"This Lord of ours is the one from whom and through whom all good things come to us."

~ST. TERESA OF ÁVILA, *AUTOBIOGRAPHY* 22, 10

READ: JOHN 8:31–41

To the Jews who believed in him Jesus said: "If you make my word your home you will indeed be my disciples, you will learn the truth and the truth will make you free." They answered, "We are descended from Abraham and we have never been the slaves of anyone; what do you mean, 'You will be made free?'" Jesus replied: "I tell you most solemnly, everyone who commits sin is a slave. Now the slave's place in the house is not assured, but the son's place is assured. So if the Son makes you free, you will be free indeed. I know that you are descended from Abraham; but in spite of that you want to kill me because nothing I say has penetrated into you. What I, for my part, speak of is what I have seen with my Father; but you, you put into action the lessons learnt from your father." They repeated, "Our father is Abraham." Jesus said to them: "If you were Abraham's children, you would do as Abraham did. As it is, you want to kill me when I tell you the truth as I have learnt it from God; that is not what Abraham did. What you are doing is what your father does."

REFLECT

Christ's word is the expression of His love. He is God, and God is love, and all His actions and words are the revelation of that love. To make His word our home, then, means to dwell in God's love for us — to relish it, to accept it, to drink it in. It involves hearing and heeding His call in our life. This call takes many forms: the nudge of conscience in little and big dilemmas; the deep, insistent, resounding invitation to a particular vocation; the normal responsibilities of life; the commandments of the Bible and of the Church. When Jesus tells us to make His word our home, He is inviting us to dwell in His will and find our comfort, our solace, our rest, and our renewal in it. Jesus comes to rescue us from our vain attempts to concoct some magic formula for self-fulfillment all by ourselves. His will is His word, and His word is the expression of His love, so to dwell in His word is to be in a constant communion with the one who loves us — to live in friendship with Christ. He is the truth, and He will set us free.

RESPOND

I believe in You, Lord. You are the one, true God. Only You are the Savior. I pray for those who don't believe in You. Show Yourself to them. Win over their hearts. Free them from sin. And what about those around me who don't believe in You? Send me to them, Lord. I want to build and spread Your Kingdom, but I need Your grace to tell me what to say, what to do, and how to love them as You have loved me.

I so easily forget that I am a fallen person in a fallen world. You have redeemed me, but You didn't take away the effects of sin. You want me to exercise my faith and love by resisting my tendencies to self-seeking and by obeying the call of Your truth. This is virtue, Lord. Virtue is freedom from the merciless and destructive slavery of self-centeredness. Teach me virtue; show me the way to go.

REST

What is Your will for me, Lord? Remind me. Life is so busy. Life is so unpredictable. Events and problems and activities swirl around me, and emotions and desires and temptations churn inside me. Make Your word alive for me. I hear and read it so often — in Mass, in spiritual reading, and in my prayer — but I want to listen better. I don't want to dwell in my paltry self, and I don't want to dwell in the passing fads of this fallen world. I want to dwell in You, in Your word, and in Your will. Teach me to do Your will.

RESOLVE

How can I carry this encounter with me into the day? (Write / Journal)

CLOSING PRAYER OF THANKSGIVING

Turn to page 9

DAY 37
THURSDAY

LIES AND DEATH, TRUTH AND LIFE

"You who have now put on Christ and follow our
guidance are like little fish on the hook: you are
being pulled up out of the deep waters of this
world by the word of God." ~ST. JEROME

READ: JOHN 8:41-59

"We were not born of prostitution," they went on, "we have one father: God."
Jesus answered: "If God were your father, you would love me, since I have
come here from God; yes, I have come from him; not that I came because I
chose, no, I was sent, and by him. Do you know why you cannot take in what
I say? It is because you are unable to understand my language. The devil is
your father, and you prefer to do what your father wants. He was a murderer
from the start; he was never grounded in the truth; there is no truth in him
at all: when he lies he is drawing on his own store, because he is a liar, and
the father of lies. But as for me, I speak the truth and for that very reason,
you do not believe me. Can one of you convict me of sin? If I speak the truth,
why do you not believe me? A child of God listens to the words of God; if
you refuse to listen, it is because you are not God's children."

The Jews replied, "Are we not right in saying that you are a Samaritan
and possessed by a devil?" Jesus answered: "I am not possessed; no, I honor
my Father, but you want to dishonor me. Not that I care for my own glory,
there is someone who takes care of that and is the judge of it. I tell you
most solemnly, whoever keeps my word will never see death." The Jews
said, "Now we know for certain that you are possessed. Abraham is dead,
and the prophets are dead, and yet you say, 'Whoever keeps my word will
never know the taste of death.' Are you greater than our father Abraham,
who is dead? The prophets are dead too. Who are you claiming to be?" Jesus
answered: "If I were to seek my own glory that would be no glory at all; my
glory is conferred by the Father, by the one of whom you say, 'He is our God,'

although you do not know him. But I know him, and if I were to say: I do not know him, I should be a liar, as you are liars yourselves. But I do know him, and I faithfully keep his word. Your father Abraham rejoiced to think that he would see my Day; he saw it and was glad." The Jews then said, "You are not fifty yet, and you have seen Abraham!" Jesus replied: "I tell you most solemnly, before Abraham ever was, I Am." At this they picked up stones to throw at him; but Jesus hid himself and left the Temple.

REFLECT

Jesus: Whoever keeps my word will never know the taste of death. Do you know what the taste of death is? It is interior darkness and the absence of hope. It is depression that gets heavier and heavier until it spawns despair. It is the sense of defeat and meaninglessness that seeps into every corner of the soul like a cold, dense fog that gets thicker and thicker and thicker. It is discovering that you are alone, that no one truly knows you, and so no one can truly love you. It is seeing the seething ugliness of sin putrefying in one's heart and being unable to do anything to wipe it away. It is watching your dreams slowly wither away, unfulfilled, or seeing them come true only to turn into nightmares as soon as you reach out to grasp them.

No one can live at peace with themselves unless they are willing to follow me. There is no other way. Death is existence without my friendship. It is what I came to destroy. You who have embraced life, you are my prize and my delight, because you let my victory in.

Keep my word, follow me, and I will give you life.

RESPOND

I have to admit, Lord, that I understand very little when it comes to the mystery of Your Incarnation. I know You are true God, and I know You are true man, but how You fit those two things together boggles my mind. But I am content to know that You who created and redeemed me continue to love and accompany me. To have God as my intimate friend is more than I could ever desire.

When I think about how much my daily decisions and actions matter in Your eyes, it fills me with enthusiasm. I can build Your Kingdom! I know that You care most about what happens in my heart. Many people build impressive worldly empires around shriveled hearts, and when their empires wane, their lives do too. But I want to live from Your love, seeking Your will, giving You glory.

REST

What would I do without Your friendship, Lord? In whom would I hope? To whom would I complain? From whom would I learn? Thank You for coming into my life. Never let me be separated from You. And fill me with Your own desire: to save many souls from death, from the hollow existence of life without Your friendship. Make me Your apostle, Your disciple, Your ambassador; make me a fisher of men.

RESOLVE

How can I carry this encounter with me into the day? (Write / Journal)

CLOSING PRAYER OF THANKSGIVING

Turn to page 9

DAY 38
FRIDAY

A SHEPHERD'S LAMENT

*"Let us have recourse to that fatherly love revealed
to us by Christ in his messianic mission, a love
which reached its culmination in his cross, in his
death and resurrection."* ~ST. JOHN PAUL II

READ: JOHN 10:19-42

These words caused disagreement among the Jews. Many said, "He is possessed, he is raving; why bother to listen to him?" Others said, "These are not the words of a man possessed by a devil: could a devil open the eyes of the blind?" It was the time when the feast of Dedication was being celebrated in Jerusalem. It was winter, and Jesus was in the Temple walking up and down in the Portico of Solomon. The Jews gathered round him and said, "How much longer are you going to keep us in suspense? If you are the Christ, tell us plainly." Jesus replied: "I have told you, but you do not believe. The works I do in my Father's name are my witness; but you do not believe, because you are no sheep of mine. The sheep that belong to me listen to my voice; I know them and they follow me. I give them eternal life; they will never be lost and no one will ever steal them from me. The Father who gave them to me is greater than anyone, and no one can steal from the Father. The Father and I are one." The Jews fetched stones to stone him, so Jesus said to them, "I have done many good works for you to see, works from my Father; for which of these are you stoning me?" The Jews answered him, "We are not stoning you for doing a good work but for blasphemy: you are only a man and you claim to be God." Jesus answered: "Is it not written in your Law: I said, you are gods? So the Law uses the word gods of those to whom the word of God was addressed, and scripture cannot be rejected. Yet you say to someone the Father has consecrated and sent into the world, 'You are blaspheming,' because he says, 'I am the son of God.' If I am not doing my Father's work, there is no need to believe me; but if I am doing it, then even if you refuse to believe in me, at least believe in the work I do; then you will know for sure that the Father is in me and I am in the Father." They wanted to arrest him then, but he eluded them. He went back again to the far side of the Jordan to stay in the district where John had once been baptizing. Many people who came to him there said, "John gave no signs, but all he said about this man was true"; and many of them believed in him.

REFLECT

"I give them eternal life." Shepherds want their sheep to thrive. They want their sheep to stay safe, to eat well, to be healthy and happy — the shepherds' livelihood depends on it. Christ is our shepherd.

> *Jesus: All I want is for you to flourish, to experience the fullness and wonder of life as I designed it to be. Every invitation I make, every indication I give through my words, my example, the commandments, the teachings of my Church, the nudges in your conscience — all have but one purpose: to lead you into the incomparably rich pastures of a life in communion with me, a communion that can begin here on earth but will reach its fulfillment only when you come home to Heaven. I want to be your Good Shepherd, and my greatest joy is when you decide to be my good sheep.*

RESPOND

You and the Father are one, and You invite me to be one with You. I can't get over how strange it is that You, Creator of all things, deign to come into my life and address me, guide me, and patiently invite me to follow You and assume responsibility in Your Kingdom. You and I both know that I don't deserve this kind of attention. It flows from Your abundant goodness, which will never run dry.

REST

You were eager to dwell among men because You had something to give them — Your love, Your wisdom, Your grace. And now You have made me Your messenger. Am I as eager as You were to engage my neighbors, to bring them Your light? I am reluctant sometimes. I don't love enough. But You know that I want to love more. And that's all You need. You will work wonders through those who trust in You.

RESOLVE

How can I carry this encounter with me into the day? (Write / Journal)

CLOSING PRAYER OF THANKSGIVING

Turn to page 9

DAY 39
SATURDAY

PAR FOR THE CHRISTIAN COURSE

"He was crucified on behalf of us all and for the sake
of us all, so that, when one had died instead of all,
we all might live in him." ~ST. CYRIL OF ALEXANDRIA

READ: JOHN 11:45-57

Many of the Jews who had come to visit Mary and had seen what he did believed in him, but some of them went to tell the Pharisees what Jesus had done. Then the chief priests and Pharisees called a meeting. "Here is this man working all these signs," they said, "and what action are we taking? If we let him go on in this way everybody will believe in him, and the Romans will come and destroy the Holy Place and our nation." One of them, Caiaphas, the high priest that year, said, "You don't seem to have grasped the situation at all; you fail to see that it is better for one man to die for the people, than for the whole nation to be destroyed." He did not speak in his own person, it was as high priest that he made this prophecy that Jesus was to die for the nation — and not for the nation only, but to gather together in unity the scattered children of God. From that day they were determined to kill him. So Jesus no longer went about openly among the Jews, but left the district for a town called Ephraim, in the country bordering on the desert, and stayed there with his disciples. The Jewish Passover drew near, and many of the country people who had gone up to Jerusalem to purify themselves looked out for Jesus, saying to one another as they stood about in the Temple, "What do you think? Will he come to the festival or not?" The chief priests and Pharisees had by now given their orders: anyone who knew where he was must inform them so that they could arrest him.

REFLECT

The Pharisees appear monstrous to us. Yet we can be just like them. When we are stuck in our sins or wallowing in self-centeredness, the good deeds of others agitate us; they prick our conscience. We try to stamp them out. We try to minimize them.

Instead of rejoicing in goodness wherever we find it, we resent it, and we rejoice instead in our neighbor's fall, since it brings him down to our level. Christ is never like that with us. The more we experience His unquenchable generosity toward us, the more it will purify our stinginess and free us to love our neighbors as He does.

> *Jesus: Do you think I despised these corrupt men who countenanced my death and scattered my sheep? How could I? They were as much my sheep as the others. They were more lost than the others, and I longed for their hearts to turn around and come to me. It was for them that I went to the Cross. They needed to see the extent of my love for them; they needed to see that nothing they could do to me was able to stop me from loving them. Rest in my heart for a moment now, and see how I love those who hate and persecute me. Since you know that I am always with you, always loving and guiding and protecting you, you have the strength to do the same.*

RESPOND

Thinking about Your providence fills my soul with peace. I know that You are always watching over me and guiding me and those around me. In some hidden way, the many Good Fridays of human history, and of my story, will all erupt into Easter Sundays. You are my Father, and in addition to loving me intensely and tenderly, You hold the reins of the universe and put everything at the service of that love.

How do I react to difficulties and opposition in life? How did You react? You accepted them, and You continued steadfastly on the path of the Father's will. Why do they upset me so much? Jesus, increase my faith.

REST

Lord Jesus, I can barely keep myself from lashing out at colleagues who show up late. How can I learn to love actual enemies, people who willfully destroy reputations and good works? And how can I refrain from criticizing those who exert their energy and influence in resisting Your action and Your Spirit? Teach me the science of the cross, Lord, and teach me the lesson of Christlike love.

RESOLVE

How can I carry this encounter with me into the day? (Write / Journal)

CLOSING PRAYER OF THANKSGIVING

Turn to page 9

DAY 40
PALM SUNDAY

LORD OF ALL, CONDEMNED BY ALL

"The Church likewise believes that the key, the center and the purpose of the whole of man's history is to be found in its Lord and Master."
~SECOND VATICAN COUNCIL, *LUMEN GENTIUM* 10

READ: MATTHEW 27:11-26

Jesus, then, was brought before the governor, and the governor put to him this question, "Are you the king of the Jews?" Jesus replied, "It is you who say it." But when he was accused by the chief priests and the elders he refused to answer at all. Pilate then said to him, "Do you not hear how many charges they have brought against you?" But to the governor's complete amazement, he offered no reply to any of the charges. At festival time it was the governor's practice to release a prisoner for the people, anyone they chose. Now there was at that time a notorious prisoner whose name was Barabbas. So when the crowd gathered, Pilate said to them, "Which do you want me to release for you: Barabbas, or Jesus who is called Christ?" For Pilate knew it was out of jealousy that they had handed him over. Now as he was seated in the chair of judgment, his wife sent him a message, "Have nothing to do with that man; I have been upset all day by a dream I had about him." The chief priests and the elders, however, had persuaded the crowd to demand the release of Barabbas and the execution of Jesus. So when the governor spoke and asked them, "Which of the two do you want me to release for you?" they said, "Barabbas." "But in that case," Pilate said to them, "what am I to do with Jesus who is called Christ?" They all said, "Let him be crucified!" "Why?" he asked. "What harm has he done?" But they shouted all the louder, "Let him be crucified!" Then Pilate saw that he was making no impression, that in fact a riot was imminent. So he took some water, washed his hands in front of the crowd and said, "I am innocent of this man's blood. It is your concern." And the people, to a man, shouted back, "His blood be on us and on our children!" Then he released Barabbas for them. He ordered Jesus to be first scourged and then handed over to be crucified.

REFLECT

Barabbas is each one of us. We are scoundrels, experts in selfishness, boasting, lust, violence, and greed. We are bandits, taking God's many gifts and ungratefully neglecting and squandering them. We take for granted the most precious realities of life: family, work, nature, health, faith, and the sacraments. We squander our talents, our money, our time, and the love others offer us. We are quick to criticize and judge, to steal others' honor and sully it with our moral and intellectual myopia. What do we, who are so flawed, so weak, so slow to repent, and so reluctant to serve — what do we deserve? Certainly not God's love, certainly not His continued forgiveness, certainly not redemption, hope, peace, and Heaven. Strictly speaking, we deserve to be cut off from the Kingdom against which we have so often rebelled — just like the murderous insurgent Barabbas.

And yet Jesus overlooks what we deserve. It is the Passover, and the angel of justice passes over the sinner to wreak his just punishments on the Lamb of God instead. Look at the Lord with the eyes of Barabbas. Is there any heart that loves you more than this Sacred Heart? Is there any heart more trustworthy than the heart that died so you might have abundant life?

RESPOND

Each day, You give me so many opportunities to choose love, to choose to act as You would act, to choose to give glory to God and further Your Kingdom by denying my selfish tendencies and putting my life and talents at the service of my neighbor. And yet, like Pilate, I squirm out of these opportunities — or like the chief priests, I self-righteously misuse them. No more, Jesus. Thy will be done.

REST

How magnificently You must love me to suffer all this for my sake! It wasn't enough to give me the universe as my sandbox; You give me Yourself as well. How can I number the gifts You have lavished upon me? Of all Your immense majesty, what moves me most is this gentle and tireless love You show me. Thank You, Lord.

RESOLVE

How can I carry this encounter with me into the day? (Write / Journal)

CLOSING PRAYER OF THANKSGIVING

Turn to page 9

MONDAY OF HOLY WEEK

THE SWEET SCENT OF LOVE

"An egg given during life for love of God is more profitable for eternity than a cathedral full of gold given after death." ~ST. ALBERT THE GREAT

READ: JOHN 12:1-11

Six days before the Passover, Jesus went to Bethany, where Lazarus was, whom he had raised from the dead. They gave a dinner for him there; Martha waited on them and Lazarus was among those at table. Mary brought in a pound of very costly ointment, pure nard, and with it anointed the feet of Jesus, wiping them with her hair; the house was full of the scent of the ointment. Then Judas Iscariot — one of his disciples, the man who was to betray him — said, "Why wasn't this ointment sold for three hundred denarii, and the money given to the poor?" He said this, not because he cared about the poor, but because he was a thief; he was in charge of the common fund and used to help himself to the contributions. So Jesus said, "Leave her alone; she had to keep this scent for the day of my burial. You have the poor with you always, you will not always have me." Meanwhile a large number of Jews heard that he was there and came not only on account of Jesus but also to see Lazarus whom he had raised from the dead. Then the chief priests decided to kill Lazarus as well, since it was on his account that many of the Jews were leaving them and believing in Jesus.

REFLECT

"Martha waited on them."

Martha: How can I describe to you that scene? Something new was in the Lord's eyes in those last days before His Passion. It was a new intensity, a new determination. Maybe "new" isn't the right word — it was just more of what had always been there: more intensity, more determination, more attention, more love. And it spread to everyone around Him. I will never forget watching Him at dinner, surrounded by His apostles, with Mary, so content, sitting at

His feet and the other guests unable to look away from Him. He was like a glowing hearth that drew in and warmed everyone around Him. His presence filled everyone with light and vigor and a freshness of life.

What the aroma of Mary's perfume was for our senses, Jesus had already been for our minds and hearts. Whenever I smell perfume now, it reminds me of the gentle power of His presence, which since then has never left me. And I knew that just as the perfume filled the house with its sweet and delicious scent, just so the Lord's life-giving presence was going to spread and fill every corner of history and the world.

RESPOND

Teach me to love You as I should, Lord. Turn me around — I don't want to keep gazing in the mirror and worrying about what others think of me and how I can achieve more than they do. I want to gaze at You, at Your truth, at the beauty of Your Kingdom. I want to care only about pouring out my life in Your service, like Mary's perfume, so that I can spread the fullness of life to those around me.

I wonder if I have it too easy, Lord. Maybe if my life were a bit less comfortable and pleasant, I would more easily remember that I am here to fulfill a mission, not just to have a good time. You lived Your life intensely, focusing on Your Father's will and the mission He had given You. And that intensity, that focus, was the source of Your joy and Your fruitfulness. Help me, Lord, to follow Your example.

REST

Lord Jesus, You have already given me so much, but I want to ask You to come anew into my life, to make me experience again the sweet aroma of Your presence. I forget so easily, Lord. The troubles of life dull my faith and hope. I need You to come and dine with me, to let me sit at Your feet and drink in Your wisdom. I want to keep fighting for Your Kingdom. Lord Jesus, give me strength.

RESOLVE

How can I carry this encounter with me into the day? (Write / Journal)

CLOSING PRAYER OF THANKSGIVING

Turn to page 9

TUESDAY OF HOLY WEEK

THE NEW COMMANDMENT

"But he was not satisfied with giving us all these beautiful things. He went to such lengths to win our love that he gave himself wholly to us. The Eternal Father gave us even his only Son." ~ST. ALPHONSUS LIGUORI

READ: JOHN 13:21-38

Having said this, Jesus was troubled in spirit and declared, "I tell you most solemnly, one of you will betray me." The disciples looked at one another, wondering which he meant. The disciple Jesus loved was reclining next to Jesus; Simon Peter signed to him and said, "Ask who it is he means," so leaning back on Jesus' breast he said, "Who is it, Lord?" "It is the one," replied Jesus, "to whom I give the piece of bread that I shall dip in the dish." He dipped the piece of bread and gave it to Judas, son of Simon Iscariot. At that instant, after Judas had taken the bread, Satan entered him. Jesus then said, "What you are going to do, do quickly." None of the others at table understood the reason he said this. Since Judas had charge of the common fund, some of them thought Jesus was telling him, "Buy what we need for the festival," or telling him to give something to the poor. As soon as Judas had taken the piece of bread he went out. Night had fallen. When he had gone Jesus said: "Now has the Son of Man been glorified, and in him God has been glorified. If God has been glorified in him, God will in turn glorify him in himself, and will glorify him very soon. My little children, I shall not be with you much longer. You will look for me, and, as I told the Jews, where I am going, you cannot come. I give you a new commandment: love one another; just as I have loved you, you also must love one another. By this love you have for one another, everyone will know that you are my disciples." Simon Peter said, "Lord, where are you going?" Jesus replied, "Where I am going you cannot follow me now; you will follow me later." Peter said to him, "Why can't I follow you now? I will lay down my life for you." "Lay down your life for me?" answered Jesus. "I tell you most solemnly, before the cock crows you will have disowned me three times."

REFLECT

If we value our friendship with Christ, we will try to please Him, make Him happy, and stay close to Him. And He (unlike many human friends) is able to tell us exactly how to do that. If we love Him, we will keep His command, and His command is for us to love one another, to put our lives at the service of those around us, just as He did for us. It is the touchstone of the Christian: "By this ... everyone will know that you are my disciples." Without it, no matter how much theology we may know, no matter how good we may be at winning arguments, no matter how many awards we may win — without learning to love as Christ has loved, we simply cannot consider ourselves His friends. When Judas left Christ to betray Him, St. John tells us that "night had fallen." It is the counterpoint to Christ's insistent self-appellation throughout the Gospel that He is the light of the world and that whoever heeds His word will not walk in darkness. Only friendship with Christ illuminates the meaning of the human condition and the path to human happiness. To reject this friendship is willingly to plunge into the darkness.

> *Jesus: I was looking ahead to my sufferings. They loomed over me. Yet I wanted them because I wanted to glorify the Father; I wanted to show forth His goodness. I wanted them, too, because of you. They would rebuild the bridge between God and man, a bridge that you could then walk across into my Kingdom. If only you knew how ardent my love for you is! That is what I wanted to show you. Let me show you. Open your mind to see the intensity of my love reflected in the intensity of my suffering.*

RESPOND

Teach me to do Your will, Lord. What more could I desire than for Your goodness to shine through my life? Your will is love and wisdom. Your will is my salvation, fulfillment, and happiness. I have only to follow Your example, the teachings of Your Church, and Your voice in my conscience. Make Your will the whole quest of my heart.

Mary, you knew all the apostles, including Judas. Why was Satan able to enter into him? I want to know. I don't trust myself. I don't want to betray Christ. Maybe I should ask instead why the others, who also abandoned

Him, were able to come back to Him. They fell because of weakness, but Judas initiated his own rebellion. Mother, save me both from weakness and from pride.

REST

Father, You sent us Your Son so that we would not have to stumble in the darkness anymore. Yet so many people continue to reject Him, and so many others have never known Him. Move their hearts, Lord. Send out messengers — convinced, courageous, determined messengers. Send me. Reach into the hearts of those around me through my words, actions, and prayers.

RESOLVE

How can I carry this encounter with me into the day? (Write / Journal)

CLOSING PRAYER OF THANKSGIVING

Turn to page 9

WEDNESDAY OF HOLY WEEK

THE TASTE OF LOVE

"I am the same under each of the species, but not every soul receives me with the same living faith as you do, my daughter, and therefore I cannot act in their souls as I do in yours." ~JESUS TO ST. FAUSTINA KOWALSKA

READ: MATTHEW 26:17-35

Now on the first day of Unleavened Bread the disciples came to Jesus to say, "Where do you want us to make the preparations for you to eat the passover?" "Go to a certain man in the city," he replied, "and say to him, 'The Master says: My time is near. It is at your house that I am keeping Passover with my disciples.'" The disciples did what Jesus told them and prepared the Passover. When evening came he was at table with the twelve disciples. And while they were eating he said, "I tell you solemnly, one of you is about to betray me." They were greatly distressed and started asking him in turn, "Not I, Lord, surely?" He answered, "Someone who has dipped his hand into the dish with me, will betray me. The Son of Man is going to his fate, as the scriptures say he will, but alas for that man by whom the Son of Man is betrayed! Better for that man if he had never been born!" Judas, who was to betray him; asked in his turn, "Not I, Rabbi, surely?" "They are your own words," answered Jesus.

Now as they were eating, Jesus took some bread, and when he had said the blessing he broke it and gave it to the disciples. "Take it and eat," he said, "this is my body." Then he took a cup, and when he had returned thanks he gave it to them. "Drink all of you from this," he said, "for this is my blood, the blood of the covenant, which is to be poured out for many for the forgiveness of sins. From now on, I tell you, I shall not drink wine until the day I drink the new wine with you in the kingdom of my Father." After psalms had been sung they left for the Mount of Olives.

Then Jesus said to them, "You will all lose faith in me this night, for the scripture says: I shall strike the shepherd and the sheep of the flock will be scattered, but after my resurrection I shall go before you to Galilee." At this, Peter said, "Though all lose faith in you, I will never lose faith." Jesus answered him, "I tell you solemnly, this very night, before the cock crows, you will have disowned me three times." Peter said to him, "Even if I have to die with you, I will never disown you." And all the disciples said the same.

REFLECT

When Jesus and His disciples celebrate this first Eucharist, the New Covenant is established. In the biblical context, a covenant is a family bond, a mutual commitment that links two parties so that they become one thing. Marriage, for example, is a covenant. God's promise to Abraham is a covenant. In establishing the New Covenant, Jesus abrogates the Mosaic Covenant, which was written on stone tablets, and fulfills Jeremiah's prophecy that after Israel's infidelity to the Old Covenant, God would make a new one — deeper, everlasting, and written on His people's hearts (see Jer. 31:31). How curious it is that St. Matthew locates the establishment of this everlasting covenant right between two predictions of betrayal, Judas's and Peter's. Jesus is willing to commit Himself to us, body and soul; He offers us His undying fidelity, even knowing we will betray Him. When He predicts the betrayals, we can hear the sadness in His voice; dipping into the same dish was a sign of close friendship, and that is how Jesus describes His betrayer, as someone close to Him, someone trusted by Him. And yet He wants His disciples to realize that He knows what will happen, so that later they will reflect on it, seeing that He loves them no matter what, even knowing their weakness. He wants to remove even the last speck of doubt from our hearts: in Christ, we have found an undying, untiring love, the firmest of anchors in the stormy sea of life.

RESPOND

Will I abandon You too, Lord? You know that I already have. So many times I have failed to trust You, I have ignored Your voice speaking in the depths of my soul. I am weak, Lord, and I am inconsistent. Be my rock; be my shield! With the fortitude of Your heart, strengthen my heart.

Your generosity humbles me, Lord! Do I deserve the great gift You give me in the Eucharist? Do I deserve the forgiveness You offer me, even before I am aware of all my sins? Do I deserve Your friendship, which You promise never to take back, even if I betray You? Do I deserve to be permitted just to speak Your Holy Name, the name that says everything? *Jesus*: "God saves." Lord Jesus, have mercy on me.

REST

I cannot receive You in the Blessed Sacrament right now, but at least come into my heart. Come to me, my Lord, and make me like You. You give without counting the cost. You love and forgive without ever demanding Your rights. I am so slow to give, so reluctant to forgive. But I know that with You I can do all things. Jesus, I trust in You.

RESOLVE

How can I carry this encounter with me into the day? (Write / Journal)

CLOSING PRAYER OF THANKSGIVING

Turn to page 9

HOLY THURSDAY

THE FINAL LESSON

"'Consider well,' he says to us, 'that in loving I was first. You had not yet come forth into the light, not even the world itself had come into existence, when already I was loving you. Throughout my eternal existence I have loved you.'" ~ST. ALPHONSUS LIGUORI

READ: JOHN 13:1-20

It was before the festival of the Passover, and Jesus knew that the hour had come for him to pass from this world to the Father. He had always loved those who were his in the world, but now he showed how perfect his love was. They were at supper, and the devil had already put it into the mind of Judas Iscariot son of Simon, to betray him. Jesus knew that the Father had put everything into his hands, and that he had come from God and was returning to God, and he got up from table, removed his outer garment and, taking a towel, wrapped it round his waist; he then poured water into a basin and began to wash the disciples' feet and to wipe them with the towel he was wearing. He came to Simon Peter, who said to him, "Lord, are you going to wash my feet?" Jesus answered, "At the moment you do not know what I am doing, but later you will understand." "Never!" said Peter. "You shall never wash my feet." Jesus replied, "If I do not wash you, you can have nothing in common with me." "Then, Lord," said Simon Peter, "not only my feet, but my hands and my head as well!" Jesus said, "No one who has taken a bath needs washing, he is clean all over. You too are clean, though not all of you are." He knew who was going to betray him, that was why he said, "Though not all of you are." When he had washed their feet and put on his clothes again he went back to the table. "Do you understand," he said, "what I have done to you? You call me Master and Lord, and rightly; so I am. If I, then, the Lord and Master, have washed your feet, you should wash each other's feet. I have given you an example so that you may copy what I have done to you. I tell you most solemnly, no servant is greater than his master, no messenger is greater than the man who sent him. Now that you know this, happiness will be yours if you behave accordingly. I am not speaking about all of you: I know the ones I have chosen; but what scripture says must be fulfilled: Someone who shares my table rebels against me. I tell you this now, before it happens, so that when it does happen you may believe that I am He. I tell you most solemnly, whoever welcomes the one I send welcomes me, and whoever welcomes me welcomes the one who sent me."

REFLECT

Judas was still at the Last Supper at this point. He had already decided to follow through with his plan of betrayal, but he had not yet left to set it in motion. What was in Jesus' mind when He came to Judas, poured water over his feet, and began to wash them? As Jesus finished drying Judas's feet with the towel, and as He laced up the sandals again, He looked into Judas's face and caught his eye. Jesus hadn't given up on him. Jesus never gives up on us; He is the ever-faithful friend. The tragedy is that we are the ones who sometimes give up on Him.

Judas: I was more disgusted than ever at this repellent display of weakness. It confirmed yet again all my suspicions: this man had come not to restore Israel to its glory but to enervate it and despoil it. I wanted nothing to do with such an imposter, such a weak dreamer. I have to admit, though, that when He looked up at me — well, it made me think of the first time we met, when I heard Him speaking in the Temple and my heart surged with hope. He had looked at me then too, and I seemed to see in His eyes all the strength and wisdom and life that I knew existed somewhere but hadn't been able to find. He invited me to come with Him then, and I couldn't resist. I had never been moved like that before. And then there were the miracles, and the huge crowds, and His mastery over the Pharisees. It was all so promising, and I could even taste victory just around the corner. But He never took the final step. And then He started talking about the cross. The others ignored it, but I knew He was serious. And how could a crucified rabbi be the Messiah? How could weakness reclaim our glory? That last night, for a split second after He replaced my sandals, it occurred to me that maybe there was more to it than I understood. But then I looked at Him again, wrapped in that towel like a slave, washing my feet. It was repugnant. Peter was right — who would ever let a real Messiah sink so low as to wash our feet? But Peter was weak too; he caved in. I could never serve a Lord like that.

RESPOND

I glory in being able to call You Lord. I know that there is order in the universe. I know that my life has purpose. I know that the world is safe in Your hands and history is marching forward according to a law of hidden progress, surely guided by Your invincible providence. Jesus, my Lord, my Master! Here is my life. I put it at Your feet and at Your service. I offer myself to You.

So many items are on my to-do list. I have so many plans and hopes. I want to do so much for You, Lord. But in the midst of my programs and activities, I too often forget about the only law of Your Kingdom: I am to wash my neighbors' feet. Only there will I ever find the happiness You intend for me. I must learn self-forgetful love. And each day, You provide so many chances for me to give myself in this way! Give me courage.

REST

You have washed my feet so often, Lord. Every time I go to Confession, You humble Yourself and wash my feet. Thank You for washing Judas's feet. I am like Judas. Have I not betrayed You at times? You knew I would; You knew my heart as You washed my feet. A Judas is within me; don't let me forget. As soon as I forget it, I will follow his example. Make me faithful, Lord; never let me be separated from You, never.

RESOLVE

How can I carry this encounter with me into the day? (Write / Journal)

CLOSING PRAYER OF THANKSGIVING

Turn to page 9

GOOD FRIDAY

A PARTING GIFT

"Mary has truly become the Mother of all believers. Men and women of every time and place have recourse to her motherly kindness and her virginal purity and grace, in all their needs and aspirations, their joys and sorrows, their moments of loneliness and their common endeavors." ~POPE BENEDICT XVI

READ: JOHN 19:17-30

Then they took charge of Jesus, and carrying his own cross he went out of the city to the place of the skull or, as it was called in Hebrew, Golgotha, where they crucified him with two others, one on either side with Jesus in the middle. Pilate wrote out a notice and had it fixed to the cross; it ran: "Jesus the Nazarene, King of the Jews." This notice was read by many of the Jews, because the place where Jesus was crucified was not far from the city, and the writing was in Hebrew, Latin and Greek. So the Jewish chief priests said to Pilate, "You should not write 'King of the Jews,' but 'This man said: I am King of the Jews.'" Pilate answered, "What I have written, I have written." When the soldiers had finished crucifying Jesus they took his clothing and divided it into four shares, one for each soldier. His undergarment was seamless, woven in one piece from neck to hem; so they said to one another, "Instead of tearing it, let's throw dice to decide who is to have it." In this way the words of scripture were fulfilled: They shared out my clothing among them. They cast lots for my clothes. This is exactly what the soldiers did. Near the cross of Jesus stood his mother and his mother's sister, Mary the wife of Clopas, and Mary of Magdala. Seeing his mother and the disciple he loved standing near her, Jesus said to his mother, "Woman, this is your son." Then to the disciple he said, "This is your mother." And from that moment the disciple made a place for her in his home. After this, Jesus knew that everything had now been completed, and to fulfill the scripture perfectly he said: "I am thirsty." A jar full of vinegar stood there, so putting a sponge soaked in the vinegar on a hyssop stick they held it up to his mouth. After Jesus had taken the vinegar he said, "It is accomplished"; and bowing his head he gave up his spirit.

REFLECT

Jesus is on the verge of completing His earthly mission. As He does so, the mission of the Church (represented in a special way by the "beloved disciple" because the Church is Jesus' beloved) is just beginning. By explicitly transferring the care of the Church (the beloved disciple) to Mary's motherly attention and entrusting Mary to John in a filial way, Jesus extends Mary's mission. She had been the Mother of Christ, the head of the Church, and now she is to be the Mother of the whole body, the members of the Church. Christ had only one thing left to give as He breathed His last breath — His own Mother, and He didn't grudge us even that. Each follower of Christ, to enter fully into God's family and to have Christ as a true brother, has to follow John's example: "And from that moment the disciple made a place for her in his home."

> Mary: I didn't choose to become Jesus' Mother; that was God's choice. How could I have ever chosen for myself such an exalted role when I always knew that I was only a blade of grass in the foothills beneath the mountain of God? Only God in His wisdom and goodness can give one of His creatures such a sublime mission. And though I didn't choose it, how much joy it gave me! Even the sorrow of His pain on Calvary filled me with a certain spiritual joy because it allowed me to suffer too; it showed Him in a new way that I would never leave Him or doubt Him. And I didn't choose to become your Mother either; that, too, was His choice. How could I have presumed to take upon myself such an exalted task — to be mother to a child born of water and the Holy Spirit? Only God in His goodness could give me such a joyful and worthy mission. And now I watch over you just as I watched over Him; I accompany you just as I accompanied Him; I love you just as I loved Him. He made me Queen of Heaven so that I could be your refuge and solace.

RESPOND

Mary, how do you guide me? I don't see your face or hear your voice. But I know you are faithful to God's will, and it is His will for you to teach and nourish me as my mother in grace. How do you do it? You instruct me by your example: you stood at the foot of the Cross, firm and faithful because your love was true and total. Teach me how to embrace fully the will of God, even when it means embracing the cross.

REST

Nothing escapes your rule, Lord. Down to the tiny detail of a hyssop stick on Calvary, You govern every speck of the cosmos and every wrinkle of human history. You are the Lord. You are my Lord. Increase my faith, Lord. I want to rejoice in the peace of knowing You more deeply and trusting You more unconditionally.

RESOLVE

How can I carry this encounter with me into the day? (Write / Journal)

CLOSING PRAYER OF THANKSGIVING

Turn to page 9

HOLY SATURDAY

THE NEW HAS COME

"Eternal life is the perfect fulfillment of desire;
inasmuch as each of the blessed will have more than
he desired or hoped for." ~ST. THOMAS AQUINAS

READ: MATTHEW 28:1-10

After the sabbath, and towards dawn on the first day of the week, Mary of Magdala and the other Mary went to visit the sepulchre. And all at once there was a violent earthquake, for the angel of the Lord, descending from heaven, came and rolled away the stone and sat on it. His face was like lightning, his robe white as snow. The guards were so shaken, so frightened of him, that they were like dead men. But the angel spoke; and he said to the women, "There is no need for you to be afraid. I know you are looking for Jesus, who was crucified. He is not here, for he has risen, as he said he would. Come and see the place where he lay, then go quickly and tell his disciples, 'He has risen from the dead and now he is going before you to Galilee; it is there you will see him.' Now I have told you." Filled with awe and great joy the women came quickly away from the tomb and ran to tell the disciples. And there, coming to meet them, was Jesus. "Greetings," he said. And the women came up to him and, falling down before him, clasped his feet. Then Jesus said to them, "Do not be afraid; go and tell my brothers that they must leave for Galilee; they will see me there."

REFLECT

For the first time in St. Matthew's Gospel, Jesus calls His apostles "my brothers." This marks a qualitative leap in their relationship with the Lord. Now that they have partaken of the Eucharist, they have Christ's own life within them; they are the first fruits of the New Covenant.

In Christ, we are no longer merely members of a chosen people, as in the Old Covenant, but we are sons with the Son; we are children of God's family; members of the household of God. Christ's restoration of communion between man and God has elevated man's dignity. This is why we sing on the Easter Vigil, "O Happy fault [the sin of Adam] that won for us so great a Redeemer!" As St. Augustine explained as the mighty Roman Empire was crumbling all around him, God permits evil only because in His wisdom, goodness, and omnipotence, He can bring an even greater good out of it. What a friend we have in Jesus!

RESPOND

You have been faithful unto death, Lord — death on a cross. And You have risen on the third day, just as You predicted. I believe in You. I put all my hopes in You. I thank You for the gift of faith. I thank You for Your saving sacrifice and Resurrection. You have promised to prepare a place for me in Heaven — my own place in Your household. Make me worthy of Your promises, Lord.

REST

Mary, how blessed was your reunion with Jesus! He is faithful, and He rewarded your fidelity. Mother, pray for me and for all Christians, that our hearts will overflow with the hope, the courage, and the assurance that only Christ can give. Cause of our joy, pray for us.

RESOLVE

How can I carry this encounter with me into the day? (Write / Journal)

CLOSING PRAYER OF THANKSGIVING

Turn to page 9

EASTER SUNDAY

THE LORD DRAWS NEAR

"This glorious son of the carpenter, who set up his
cross above the all-consuming world of the dead, led
the human race into the abode of life." ~ST. EPHRAEM

READ: LUKE 24:13-35

That very same day, two of them were on their way to a village called Emmaus, seven miles from Jerusalem, and they were talking together about all that had happened. Now as they talked this over, Jesus himself came up and walked by their side; but something prevented them from recognising him. He said to them, "What matters are you discussing as you walk along?" They stopped short, their faces downcast. Then one of them, called Cleopas, answered him, "You must be the only person staying in Jerusalem who does not know the things that have been happening there these last few days." "What things?" he asked. "All about Jesus of Nazareth," they answered, "who proved he was a great prophet by the things he said and did in the sight of God and of the whole people; and how our chief priests and our leaders handed him over to be sentenced to death, and had him crucified. Our own hope had been that he would be the one to set Israel free. And this is not all: two whole days have gone by since it all happened; and some women from our group have astounded us: they went to the tomb in the early morning, and when they did not find the body, they came back to tell us they had seen a vision of angels who declared he was alive. Some of our friends went to the tomb and found everything exactly as the women had reported, but of him they saw nothing."

Then he said to them, "You foolish men! So slow to believe the full message of the prophets! Was it not ordained that the Christ should suffer and so enter into his glory?" Then, starting with Moses and going through all the prophets, he explained to them the passages throughout the scriptures that were about himself. When they drew near to the village to which they were going, he made as if to go on; but they pressed him to stay with them. "It is nearly evening," they said, "and the day is almost over." So he went in to stay with them. Now while he was with them at table, he took the bread and said the blessing; then he broke it and handed it to them. And their eyes were opened and they recognised him; but he had vanished from their sight. Then they said to each other, "Did not our hearts burn within us as he talked to us on the road and explained the scriptures to us?" They set out that instant and returned to Jerusalem. There they found the Eleven assembled together with their companions, who said to them, "Yes, it is true. The Lord has risen and has appeared to Simon." Then they told their story of what had happened on the road and how they had recognised him at the breaking of bread.

REFLECT

"Jesus himself came up and walked by their side." Christ continues to do this every day in the Blessed Sacrament. In every Mass, in every tabernacle, He draws near to us and walks by our side. In Holy Communion, He continues to share His life with us. He is truly present, reaching out to us, speaking to our hearts, behind the thin veil of faith. If only we, like these two disciples, are honest and courageous enough to open our hearts to Him and invite Him into the secret places of our souls, we will see Him anew, and His love will burn within us.

> *Jesus: I know when you are downcast and sad. I know when the shadow of the Cross and Good Friday make you turn away from Jerusalem and head back to your old ways. I know, and I care, more than you can imagine. I am always drawing near to you. I speak in the quiet voice of your conscience, where only you can hear me. Sometimes I speak to you through the words of a friend or a verse from the Bible. Whenever you hear my voice, and you know when you do, you have only to welcome it, to make your prayer the same as that of these two disciples, who pressed me to stay with them. Will I ever deny such a request, I who came all the way down from Heaven just because I couldn't stand being far away from you? This is why I came; this is why I died; this is why I rose again — to stay with you.*

RESPOND

I have chosen to follow You, Lord, and no one else. I know it's only because You called me, but I have made the choice. You didn't force me. And I want to be true to that choice. You are the Lord. You are the fount of wisdom, forgiveness, love, and life that fills the world with whatever goodness it has. Make me a channel of Your grace, a riverbed for Your flowing fountain.

The struggles of my life seem so irrelevant sometimes when I go to Mass. But how could they be? Do You not care about them? Dear Lord, it's a mystery to me, this passing life, so busy but so out of focus. Help me to know in each moment what I should do and how I should be. I have only this life to live, and I want to live it well.

REST

Stay with me, Lord. How I need a friend who knows me through and through and doesn't judge me! How I need a coach who knows my strengths and weaknesses and who knows how to profit from the former and shore up the latter! I feel such a burning desire to do something worthwhile, to do more — You put that desire in my heart. Now show me what to do with it.

RESOLVE

How can I carry this encounter with me into the day? (Write / Journal)

CLOSING PRAYER OF THANKSGIVING

Turn to page 9

WHAT'S NEXT

Congratulations! You are now well on your way to a life-changing habit of daily mental prayer that will bring you peace and help you to know the God of peace in these challenging times. If you are like most people, you may have run into challenges during your forty-day adventure, or you may have questions about progress in prayer. Here are a handful of powerful resources we recommend to help you navigate your way into the depths of your relationship with God:

Into the Deep video series: If you did not already utilize this course and would like to take a powerful course on mental prayer from Dan Burke go to: https://spiritualdirection.com/into-the-deep.

The Better Part: A Christ-Centered Resource for Personal Prayer: This book is the source of the reflections you enjoyed during these forty days. Dan Burke has indicated that there is no better book ever published for daily reflections on the four Gospels. You can find these in four volumes at SpiritualDirection.com or at SophiaInstitute.com. Use the coupon code BetterPart20 at SophiaInstitute.com to get 20 percent off *The Better Part* — the four-volume set or each of the individual four volumes. Good through the end of May 2023!

Into the Deep: Finding Peace through Prayer: This book by Dan Burke will solidify your foundations in prayer and the method of prayer that was used in this Lenten resource and will help you overcome common obstacles to growth in prayer. It is a quick read that most find very helpful and enriching to their prayer life. You can find this book at SpiritualDirection.com.

Foundations of Prayer and Union with God: a full live online course on the depths of prayer, taught by Dan Burke: This course has helped laity, priests, and religious to deepen their love of prayer and to better understand how to know the heights of prayer and contemplation that God desires all to experience. The course is available at Avila-Institute.org.

Digital mini retreats on the interior life offered by Fr. John Bartunek: These can be found at RCSpirituality.org. Fr. John is a dynamic and faithful teacher of authentic Catholic spirituality and one of the most trustworthy sources of spiritual formation in our time.

Vibrant Catholic community: If you are looking to escape the dark world of social media and enter into the encouraging and vibrant life of authentic Catholic community, check out ApostoliViae.org. You will be able to join bimonthly formation on the second and fourth Saturdays of each month as you continue to grow deeper on your faith journey. This joyful orthodox Catholic community is dedicated to serving you as you seek to know and follow God in your life.

MY NOTES

MY NOTES

MY NOTES

MY NOTES

MY NOTES

MY NOTES

MY NOTES

MY NOTES

MY NOTES

MY NOTES

MY NOTES

MY NOTES

MY NOTES

Sophia Institute

Sophia Institute is a nonprofit institution that seeks to nurture the spiritual, moral, and cultural life of souls and to spread the Gospel of Christ in conformity with the authentic teachings of the Roman Catholic Church.

Sophia Institute Press fulfills this mission by offering translations, reprints, and new publications that afford readers a rich source of the enduring wisdom of mankind.

Sophia Institute also operates the popular online resource CatholicExchange.com. *Catholic Exchange* provides world news from a Catholic perspective as well as daily devotionals and articles that will help readers to grow in holiness and live a life consistent with the teachings of the Church.

In 2013, Sophia Institute launched Sophia Institute for Teachers to renew and rebuild Catholic culture through service to Catholic education. With the goal of nurturing the spiritual, moral, and cultural life of souls, and an abiding respect for the role and work of teachers, we strive to provide materials and programs that are at once enlightening to the mind and ennobling to the heart; faithful and complete, as well as useful and practical.

Sophia Institute gratefully recognizes the Solidarity Association for preserving and encouraging the growth of our apostolate over the course of many years. Without their generous and timely support, this book would not be in your hands.

www.SophiaInstitute.com
www.CatholicExchange.com
www.SophiaInstituteforTeachers.org

Sophia Institute Press˙ is a registered trademark of Sophia Institute.
Sophia Institute is a tax-exempt institution as defined by the
Internal Revenue Code, Section 501(c)(3). Tax ID 22-2548708.